Indulgence
food

UK COOKERY EDITOR
Katie Swallow

EDITORIAL
Food Editor: Sheryle Eastwood
Assistant Food Editor: Anneka Mitchell
Home Economist: Donna Hay
Editorial Coordinator: Margaret Kelly
Recipe development: Penny Cox, Elise Pascoe,
Anna Philips

PHOTOGRAPHY
Andrew Payne

STYLING
Rosemary De Santis

COVER DESIGN
Frank Pithers

DESIGN AND PRODUCTION
Manager: Nadia Sbisa
Senior Production Editor: Rachel Blackmore
Design and Layout: Margie Mulray
Finished Art: Chris Hatcher

PUBLISHER
Philippa Sandall

Includes Index
ISBN 1 86343 023 7

Family Circle is a registered tradedmark
of IPC Magazines Ltd
Published by J. B. Fairfax Press Pty Ltd by
arrangement with IPC Magazines Ltd

Formatted by J.B. Fairfax Press Pty Ltd
Output by Adytype, Sydney
Printed by Toppan Printing Co, Hong Kong

Distributed by J. B. Fairfax Press Ltd
9 Trinity Centre, Park Farm Estate
Wellingborough, Northants
Ph: (0933) 402330 Fax: (0933) 402234

CONTENTS

MICROWAVE IT

Where microwave instructions occur in this book a microwave oven with a 650 watt output has been used. Wattage on domestic microwave ovens varies between 500 and 700 watts, so it may be necessary to vary the cooking times slightly depending on the wattage of your oven.

CHECK-AND-GO

Use the easy Check-and-Go boxes which appear beside each ingredient. Simply check your pantry and if the ingredients are not there, tick the boxes as a reminder to add those items to your shopping list.

CANNED FOODS

Can sizes vary between countries and manufacturers. You may find the quantities in this book are slightly different to what is available. Purchase and use the can size nearest to the suggested size in the recipe.

METRIC CUPS & SPOONS

Metric	Cups	Imperial
60 mL	¼ cup	2 fl oz
80 mL	⅓ cup	2½ fl oz
125 mL	½ cup	4 fl oz
250 mL	1 cup	8 fl oz
	Spoons	
1.25 mL	¼ teaspoon	
2.5 mL	½ teaspoon	
5 mL	1 teaspoon	
20 mL	1 tablespoon	

WICKEDLY DELICIOUS

Devoted to delicious desserts and cakes, this chapter looks elaborate but, even so, don't think that everything in it is hard to make. All the recipes are simple to follow and with a little care your efforts will look just like the photographs.

CHOCOLATE MUD CAKE WITH CHOCOLATE SAUCE

Whatever the occasion for the true chocoholic, this cake with its rich chocolate sauce is a party in itself.

Serves 10-12
Oven temperature 120°C, 250°F, Gas ½

- [ ] **250 g (8 oz) butter, cubed**
- [ ] **300 g (9½ oz) dark chocolate, broken into small pieces**
- [ ] **5 eggs, separated**
- [ ] **2 tablespoons caster sugar**
- [ ] **3 tablespoons self-raising flour, sifted**
- [ ] **whipped cream**

RICH CHOCOLATE SAUCE
- [ ] **200 g (6½ oz) dark chocolate, broken into small pieces**
- [ ] **75 g (2½ oz) unsalted butter**
- [ ] **170 g (5½ oz) caster sugar**
- [ ] **4 tablespoons cocoa powder, sifted**
- [ ] **4 tablespoons milk**
- [ ] **4 tablespoons double cream**

1 Melt butter and chocolate in a bowl over simmering water, stirring until melted and smooth. Remove bowl and allow chocolate mixture to cool slightly.

2 Beat egg yolks and sugar into chocolate mixture then fold in flour.

3 Place egg whites in a mixing bowl and beat until stiff peaks form. Fold lightly into chocolate mixture. Pour into a greased and lined 20 cm (8 in) round cake tin. Bake for 1¼ hours, or until cooked when tested with a skewer. Turn off oven and cool cake in oven with door ajar.

4 To make sauce, place chocolate and butter in a bowl over a saucepan of simmering water until melted. Stir in sugar and cocoa powder and mix to combine. Add milk and cream and heat for 5 minutes longer, stirring occasionally. Remove pan from heat and pour sauce into a jug. Set aside to cool. Serve cake with sauce and cream.

Chocolate Mud Cake with Chocolate Sauce

China Wedgewood

BERRY STACKS WITH RASPBERRY COULIS

Serves 6
Oven temperature 190°C, 375°F, Gas 5

- [ ] **2 egg whites**
- [ ] **100 g (3½ oz) caster sugar**
- [ ] **60 g (2 oz) butter, melted and cooled**
- [ ] **60 g (2 oz) plain flour, sifted**
- [ ] **1 tablespoon dark rum**
- [ ] **icing sugar**

FILLING
- [ ] **1 egg, lightly beaten**
- [ ] **3 tablespoons caster sugar**
- [ ] **1½ tablespoons cornflour**
- [ ] **1 teaspoon vanilla essence**
- [ ] **170 mL (5½ fl oz) milk, scalded**
- [ ] **15 g (½ oz) butter**
- [ ] **250 mL (8 fl oz) double cream, whipped**
- [ ] **375 g (12 oz) small strawberries, hulled and halved**
- [ ] **375 g (12 oz) blueberries**

RASPBERRY COULIS
- [ ] **250 g (8 oz) raspberries**
- [ ] **1 tablespoon caster sugar**
- [ ] **2 tablespoons Framboise (raspberry liqueur)**

1   Beat egg whites until soft peaks form. Add sugar a little at a time, beating well after each addition until mixture is thick and glossy. Add butter and beat. Fold in flour and rum.

2   Place 24 spoonfuls of mixture onto greased and lined baking trays and spread to form thin 7.5 cm (3 in) circles. Bake for 6-8 minutes, or until a light golden colour. Allow to cool on trays.

3   To make filling, combine egg, sugar, cornflour and vanilla essence in a saucepan. Whisk in milk and stir over a low heat until mixture is smooth and thickens. Beat in butter and set aside to cool, then fold in cream.

4   To make coulis, place raspberries, sugar and liqueur in a food processor or blender and process until smooth.

5   To assemble, place a biscuit circle on each serving plate, spoon a little filling over and top with strawberries and blueberries. Repeat layers using four biscuit circles, finishing with a biscuit circle. Serve with coulis. Dust with sifted icing sugar.

BERRY CHARLOTTE

Serves 6

- [ ] **9 sponge fingers**
- [ ] **9 striped biscuit wafers**

FILLING
- [ ] **220 g (7 oz) unsalted butter, softened**
- [ ] **170 g (5½ oz) caster sugar**
- [ ] **2 tablespoons dark rum**
- [ ] **185 g (6 oz) ground almonds**
- [ ] **315 mL (10 fl oz) thickened cream**
- [ ] **440 g (14 oz) canned blackberries, drained**
- [ ] **440 g (14 oz) canned raspberries, drained**

COOK'S TIP
Fresh blackberries and raspberries make the Berry Charlotte even more indulgent. If using fresh berries use 250 g (8 oz) blackberries and 250 g (8 oz) raspberries.

China Limoges *Silverwear* Oneida

1   Arrange sponge fingers and wafers alternately around the sides of a greased and foil-lined 18 cm (7 in) springform cake tin, trimming bottom end of sponge fingers to fit if necessary.

2   To make filling, beat butter and sugar until light and fluffy. Add rum and ground almonds and beat well. Whip cream until soft peaks form. Fold into almond mixture.

3   Spoon one-third of mixture into prepared tin and arrange drained blackberries evenly over top. Spoon another third of mixture over blackberries and top evenly with drained raspberries. Spoon remaining mixture over raspberries. Refrigerate overnight or until firm. To serve, remove from pan and arrange on a serving platter. Tie ribbon decoratively around outside of charlotte.

Below: Berry Stacks with Raspberry Coulis, Berry Charlotte
Right: Blissful Chocolate Bombe

Plate Incorporated Agencies

❧
BLISSFUL CHOCOLATE BOMBE

Serves 12

VANILLA ICE CREAM
- [ ] **220 g (7 oz) caster sugar**
- [ ] **8 egg yolks**
- [ ] **660 mL (22 fl oz) single cream**
- [ ] **1 vanilla pod**
- [ ] **375 mL (12 fl oz) double cream**

CHOCOLATE MOUSSE
- [ ] **170 g (5¹/₂ oz) dark chocolate, broken into small pieces**
- [ ] **3 tablespoons strong black coffee**
- [ ] **4 eggs, separated**
- [ ] **15 g (¹/₂ oz) butter, softened**
- [ ] **1 tablespoon brandy**
- [ ] **3 tablespoons caster sugar**
- [ ] **125 mL (4 fl oz) double cream, whipped**

1   To make ice cream, place sugar and egg yolks in a bowl and beat until thick and creamy. Place single cream and vanilla pod in a heavy-based saucepan and simmer for 3 minutes. Cool slightly, then remove vanilla pod.

2   Gradually add 250 mL (8 fl oz) of warm cream to egg mixture, beating well. Add egg mixture to remaining cream, stirring over low heat until mixture coats the back of a spoon. Set aside to cool.

3   Stir in double cream, pour into a freezerproof tray lined with plastic food wrap, and freeze until almost set. Break up mixture with a fork and place in food processor. Process until mixture is thick and creamy. Pour ice cream into a chilled mould (2.25 litre/3³/₄ pt capacity) lined with plastic food wrap. Push a smaller mould, covered with plastic food wrap, into centre of ice cream, forcing ice cream up around the sides of the mould. Freeze until firm.

4   To make chocolate mousse, place chocolate and coffee in a bowl and melt over a saucepan of simmering water, stirring until smooth. Remove from heat and beat in egg yolks one at a time. Continue beating and add butter and brandy. Allow mixture to cool.

5   Beat egg whites until soft peaks form, then beat in sugar. Fold egg whites and cream into chocolate mixture. Remove smaller mould from ice cream. Spoon mousse into centre of ice cream and return to freezer until set.

STRIPED ROULADE WITH APRICOT MOUSSE FILLING

This impressive roulade may look very grand but it is in fact easy to make. Follow our step-by-step recipe and see just how easy it really is.

Serves 6
Oven temperature 200°C, 400°F, Gas 6

- ☐ **60 g (2 oz) self-raising flour, sifted**
- ☐ **2 tablespoons cocoa, sifted**
- ☐ **4 eggs**
- ☐ **5 tablespoons caster sugar**

APRICOT MOUSSE FILLING
- ☐ **1 tablespoon gelatine**
- ☐ **3 tablespoons orange juice**
- ☐ **440 g (14 oz) canned apricots, drained and 3 tablespoons liquid reserved**
- ☐ **3 eggs, separated**
- ☐ **4 tablespoons caster sugar**
- ☐ **1 tablespoon brandy**
- ☐ **1 tablespoon Cointreau (orange liqueur)**
- ☐ **125 mL (4 fl oz) double cream**

1 Place 2 tablespoons flour and cocoa in a mixing bowl and the remaining flour in another.

2 Beat eggs and sugar until thick and creamy. Divide mixture evenly between two bowls. Fold cocoa mixture into egg mixture in one bowl and fold flour mixture into the remaining egg mixture.

3 Place chocolate and plain cake batters into two separate piping bags fitted with 1.5 cm (³/₄ in) plain nozzles. Pipe lines of chocolate mixture 1.5 cm (³/₄ in) apart diagonally across a greased and lined Swiss roll tin. Then pipe plain mixture in lines between chocolate strips. Bake for 8-10 minutes, or until cake is cooked through and springy to touch.

4 Turn roulade out onto a damp teatowel sprinkled with caster sugar. Roll up sponge with aid of teatowel from short end and allow to cool.

5 To make filling, sprinkle gelatine over orange juice in a small bowl, place over a small saucepan of simmering water and stir until gelatine dissolves. Set aside to cool at room temperature. Place apricots and reserved liquid in a food processor or blender and process until smooth. Beat egg yolks and sugar in a bowl until thick and creamy. Stir in apricot purée, gelatine

mixture, brandy and Cointreau. Beat cream until soft peaks form, fold into apricot mixture. Beat egg whites until soft peaks form, fold into apricot mixture. Refrigerate for 2-3 hours, or until mixture is almost set. Unroll roulade and spread with filling. Re-roll and refrigerate until filling is set.

Pipe lines of chocolate mixture 1.5 cm (³/₄ in) apart diagonally across a greased and lined Swiss roll tin. Then pipe plain mixture between chocolate stripes.

Turn roulade onto a damp teatowel sprinkled with caster sugar, and roll up from short end.

Unroll roulade, spread with filling, and re-roll. Refrigerate until filling is set.

Props Accoutrement

9

China Limoges *Silverware* Oneida

Chocolate Meringue Cake

❧
ORANGE AND DATE GATEAU

Serves 8
Oven temperature 180°C, 350°F, Gas 4

- ☐ **4 eggs**
- ☐ **100 g (3½ oz) caster sugar**
- ☐ **60 g (2 oz) plain flour, sifted**
- ☐ **4 tablespoons self-raising flour, sifted**
- ☐ **orange slices**

ORANGE AND DATE FILLING
- ☐ **1 tablespoon brandy**
- ☐ **1 tablespoon Cointreau (orange liqueur)**
- ☐ **155 g (5 oz) fresh dates, pitted and chopped**
- ☐ **3 tablespoons sugar**
- ☐ **125 mL (4 fl oz) water**
- ☐ **1 orange, peeled and chopped**
- ☐ **1 egg, lightly beaten**
- ☐ **3 tablespoons caster sugar**
- ☐ **1½ tablespoons cornflour**
- ☐ **170 mL (5½ fl oz) milk, scalded**
- ☐ **250 mL (8 fl oz) double cream**

TOFFEE
- ☐ **100 g (3½ oz) caster sugar**
- ☐ **100 g (3½ oz) muscovado sugar**
- ☐ **1 tablespoon coffee sugar crystals**

ORANGE BUTTERCREAM TOPPING
- ☐ **3 egg yolks**
- ☐ **3 tablespoons caster sugar**
- ☐ **4 tablespoons milk, scalded**
- ☐ **2 drops orange food colouring, optional**
- ☐ **155 g (5 oz) icing sugar, sifted**
- ☐ **185 g (6 oz) unsalted butter, softened**

1   Beat eggs and sugar in a mixing bowl, until mixture is thick and creamy and forms a ribbon. Fold in plain and self-raising flours. Pour mixture into a greased and lined 20 cm (8 in) cake tin and bake for 25-30 minutes, or until cooked through and golden. Stand in cake tin for 5 minutes before turning out onto a wire rack to cool.
2   To make filling, place brandy, Cointreau and dates in a bowl and set aside to stand for 30 minutes. Place sugar and water in a small saucepan and cook over a low heat, stirring constantly, until sugar dissolves. Add oranges, bring to the boil, then reduce heat and simmer for 20 minutes. Remove from heat and set aside to cool.
3   Drain oranges and add to date mixture. Combine egg, sugar and cornflour in a

❧
CHOCOLATE MERINGUE CAKE

Serves 10
Oven temperature 120°C, 250°F, Gas ½

HAZELNUT MERINGUE
- ☐ **155 g (5 oz) hazelnuts, ground**
- ☐ **2 tablespoons cornflour**
- ☐ **310 g (10 oz) caster sugar**
- ☐ **6 egg whites**
- ☐ **whipped cream**

CHOCOLATE FILLING
- ☐ **220 g (7 oz) unsalted butter**
- ☐ **185 g (6 oz) dark chocolate, melted**
- ☐ **3 tablespoons caster sugar**
- ☐ **500 mL (16 fl oz) double cream**
- ☐ **2 tablespoons brandy**
- ☐ **125 g (4 oz) hazelnuts, ground**

CHOCOLATE TOPPING
- ☐ **155 g (5 oz) dark chocolate**
- ☐ **2 teaspoons vegetable oil**

1   To make meringue, combine ground hazelnuts, cornflour and 185 g (6 oz) sugar. Beat egg whites until soft peaks form, add remaining sugar a little at a time and beat until thick and glossy. Fold into hazelnut mixture.
2   Mark three 20 cm (8 in) squares on baking paper and place on baking trays. Place meringue mixture in a piping bag fitted with a small plain nozzle and pipe mixture to outline squares, then fill centres with piped lines of mixture. Bake for 40-50 minutes, or until crisp and dry.
3   To make filling, beat butter until soft. Add chocolate, caster sugar and cream and beat until thick. Fold in brandy and hazelnuts.
4   To make topping, place chocolate and oil in a bowl over a saucepan of simmering water, stirring until chocolate melts and mixture is smooth. Remove bowl and set aside to cool.
5   To assemble cake, place a layer of meringue on a serving plate and spread with half the filling. Top with another meringue layer and remaining filling. Cut remaining meringue into squares and position at angles on top of cake. Drizzle with topping and decorate with cream.

10

saucepan, whisk in milk and cook over a low heat, stirring until mixture is smooth and thickens. Set aside to cool. Beat cream until soft peaks form. Fold in dates and oranges.

4   To make toffee, sprinkle caster sugar, muscovado sugar and coffee crystals on an oven tray covered with greased foil. Place under a preheated hot grill and cook until sugar caramelises and melts into a thin sheet. Watch closely, as the sugar burns easily. Set aside to cool. Break into pieces.

5   To assemble gâteau, cut cake horizontally into three layers. Spread bottom layer with half the filling, top with second layer of cake, and spread with remaining filling. Top with remaining cake layer and refrigerate for 30 minutes.

6   To make buttercream, beat egg yolks and sugar until thick and creamy and mixture forms a ribbon when whisk is lifted. Whisk in scalded milk and pour mixture into a bowl and cook over a saucepan of simmering water until mixture thickens and coats the back of a wooden spoon. Stir in food colouring if using and set aside to cool. Place mixture in a mixing bowl and beat in icing sugar and butter a little at a time until mixture is creamy and stiff peaks form. Spread evenly over sides and top of cake. Decorate with toffee pieces and orange slices.

❧

STEAMED PEAR PUDDING WITH CARAMEL SAUCE

Serves 8

- ☐ **3 pears, peeled, cored and finely chopped**
- ☐ **125 mL (4 fl oz) water**
- ☐ **1¹/₂ tablespoons sugar**
- ☐ **45 g (1¹/₂ oz) butter**
- ☐ **3 tablespoons caster sugar**
- ☐ **2 eggs**
- ☐ **90 g (3 oz) self-raising flour, sifted**
- ☐ **4 tablespoons milk**

CARAMEL SAUCE
- ☐ **185 g (6 oz) sugar**
- ☐ **3 tablespoons water**
- ☐ **45 g (1¹/₂ oz) unsalted butter, cut into pieces**
- ☐ **155 mL (5 fl oz) double cream**

1   Place pears, water and sugar in a saucepan and cook over a medium heat for 10 minutes, or until pears are just tender. Remove from heat and set aside.

2   Cream butter and caster sugar until pale and fluffy. Add eggs and beat well. Sift flour over mixture and fold in with milk.

3   Strain pears and fold into pudding mixture. Pour into a greased 1¹/₂ litre (3 pt) capacity pudding basin. Cover with a round of lightly greased baking paper, then foil and pudding basin lid.

4   Place basin in a large saucepan with enough boiling water to come halfway up the side of the basin. Boil for 1¹/₂ hours, or until pudding is firm, replacing water if necessary as the pudding cooks. Allow to stand 5 minutes before turning out.

5   To make sauce, place sugar and water together in a heavy-based saucepan and cook over a medium heat, stirring until sugar dissolves. Cook until mixture caramelises and is a deep amber colour. Remove from heat. Add butter one piece at a time, stirring until melted. Return sauce to heat, pour in cream and cook, stirring, for 2 minutes. Remove from heat and set aside to cool. Serve with pudding.

Steamed Pear Pudding with Caramel Sauce, Orange and Date Gâteau

CHOCOHOLIC

The source of chocolate, the cacao tree, was one of the greatest discoveries made on the American continent. Chocolate's smooth, rich flavour is loved by almost everyone. Its scientific name is *Theobroma cacao* (*theobroma* means 'food of the gods').

Storing chocolate

Chocolate should be stored in a dry, airy place at a temperature of about 16°C (52°F). If stored in unsuitable conditions, the cocoa butter in chocolate may rise to the surface, leaving a white bloom. A similar discolouration occurs when water condenses on the surface. This often happens to refrigerated chocolates that are too loosely wrapped. Chocolate affected this way is still suitable for melting, however it is unsuitable for grating.

Melting chocolate

Chocolate melts more rapidly if broken into small pieces. The melting process should occur slowly, as chocolate scorches if overheated. To melt chocolate, place it in a bowl over a pan of hot, not boiling, water and set aside. The water should not touch the bowl. Stand off the heat, stirring occasionally until chocolate melts and is of a smooth consistency. Alternatively, melt in a double saucepan. Cool at room temperature.

Watchpoints

❦ Do not melt chocolate over a direct flame.

❦ The container in which the chocolate is being melted should be kept uncovered and completely dry. Covering could cause condensation and just one drop of water will ruin the chocolate.

❦ Chocolate 'seizes' if it is over-heated, or if it comes into contact with water or steam. Seizing results in the chocolate tightening and becoming a thick mass that will not melt. To rescue seized chocolate, stir in a little cream, vegetable oil or a knob of butter, until the chocolate becomes smooth again.

Compound chocolate

Compound chocolate, also called chocolate coating, is designed to replace couverture chocolate for coating. It can be purchased in block form or as round discs. Both forms are available in milk or dark chocolate. Compound chocolate is made from a vegetable oil base with sugar, milk

solids and flavouring. It contains cocoa powder, but not cocoa butter and is easy to melt. It does not require tempering and is the easiest form for beginners to work with.

Chocolate Decorations

Chocolate caraque: Pour melted chocolate over a cool work surface such as marble, ceramic or granite. Spread the chocolate as smoothly as possible, using a flexible metal spatula, in a thin layer; do not leave any holes. If the chocolate is too thick it will not curl. Allow chocolate to set at room temperature. Holding a long sharp knife at a 45° angle, pull gently over the surface of the chocolate to form scrolls.

Chocolate curls and shavings: Chocolate curls are made from chocolate that is at room temperature. To make shavings, chill the chocolate first. Using a vegetable peeler, shave the sides of the chocolate. Curls or shavings will form depending on the temperature of the chocolate.

Chocolate leaves: Use stiff, fresh, non-poisonous leaves such as rose leaves. Keep as much stem as possible to hold onto. Wash and dry leaves, brush the shiny surface of the leaf with a thin layer of melted, cooled chocolate. Allow to set at room temperature then carefully peel away leaf.

Piping chocolate: Chocolate can be piped into fancy shapes for decorating desserts or cakes. Trace a simple design on a thin piece of paper. Tape a sheet of greaseproof paper to the work surface and slide the drawing under the sheet of paper. Pipe over outline with melted chocolate. Set aside to firm at room temperature, then remove carefully with a spatula and use as desired.

Chocolates cases: Pour melted chocolate into paper cake cases to quarter-fill, then tap to remove any air bubbles. Brush chocolate evenly up sides of cake cases, then freeze for 2 minutes or until set. Larger chocolate cases to hold desserts can also be made in this way using foil-lined individual metal flan tins, brioche or muffin tins as moulds. When set, remove from tins and fill with a dessert filling such as mousse or a flavoured cream.

CHOCOLATE MOCHA CAKE

A rich chocolate cake that could easily become a favourite. Decorate with chocolate leaves, curls or piped decorations to make an extra-special adult birthday cake.

Serves 8
Oven temperature 160°C, 325°F, Gas 3

- ☐ **185 g (6 oz) dark chocolate, broken into small pieces**
- ☐ **4 eggs, separated**
- ☐ **100 g (3¹/₂ oz) caster sugar**
- ☐ **185 g (6 oz) unsalted butter, softened and cut into pieces**
- ☐ **2 tablespoons strong black coffee**
- ☐ **60 g (2 oz) plain flour, sifted**

CHOCOLATE GLAZE
- ☐ **200 g (6¹/₂ oz) dark chocolate, broken into small pieces**
- ☐ **100 g (3¹/₂ oz) unsalted butter**
- ☐ **2 tablespoons water**

1 Place chocolate in a bowl over a saucepan of simmering water for 5 minutes, or until chocolate melts. Remove bowl from heat and stir until smooth. Set aside to cool.

2 Place egg yolks and sugar in a bowl and beat until pale and fluffy. Add butter and beat mixture until creamy. Add coffee and chocolate and continue beating mixture until creamy. Sift flour over mixture and fold in lightly.

3 Beat egg whites until soft peaks form. Lightly fold egg white mixture into chocolate mixture. Pour into a greased and lined 20 cm (8 in) cake tin and bake for 30 minutes, or until firm to touch. Turn off oven and cool cake in oven with door ajar. Remove from tin and refrigerate for 2 hours or overnight.

4 To make glaze, place chocolate, butter and water in a bowl over a saucepan of simmering water until chocolate and butter melt. Remove bowl from heat and stir ingredients to combine. Set aside to cool and thicken.

5 Remove cake from refrigerator and place on a wire rack. Place on a tray and pour glaze over cake, smoothing it over edges and onto sides with a spatula. Leave until completely set. Transfer cake to a flat serving plate and cut into slices to serve.

Chocolate Mocha Cake

Variation

For chocoholics this cake can be made even more special if you make two cakes, then sandwich them together with whipped cream and decorate the top with chocolate caraques (see page 12).

APPLE AND MASCARPONE STACKS

Serves 4
Oven temperature 180°C, 350°F, Gas 4

- ☐ **8 sheets filo pastry**
- ☐ **90 g (3 oz) butter, melted**
- ☐ **4 tablespoons caster sugar**
- ☐ **60 g (2 oz) ground almonds**

APPLE FILLING
- ☐ **250 g (8 oz) sugar**
- ☐ **125 mL (4 fl oz) water**
- ☐ **2 green apples, peeled, cored and thinly sliced**
- ☐ **3 tablespoons Calvados (apple brandy)**

MASCARPONE PRALINE FILLING
- ☐ **4 tablespoons flaked almonds, toasted**
- ☐ **2 tablespoons Calvados (apple brandy)**
- ☐ **500 g (1 lb) mascarpone or cream cheese**

TOFFEE SAUCE
- ☐ **155 mL (5 fl oz) double cream**
- ☐ **90 g (3 oz) butter**
- ☐ **125 g (4 oz) brown sugar**

1   Layer 4 sheets of pastry (keeping remaining pastry covered), brushing between each pastry layer with butter and sprinkling with a little sugar and almonds. Press layers together to seal, then cut into 7.5 cm (3 in) squares. Repeat with remaining pastry, butter, sugar and almonds. Place pastry squares onto greased oven trays and bake for 10-12 minutes.

2   To make Apple Filling, place sugar and water in a saucepan and cook over a low heat, stirring until sugar dissolves. Add apples and Calvados and cook until tender. Drain apples and reserve liquid.

3   To make Mascarpone Praline Filling, place reserved apple liquid in a clean pan and simmer until golden and syrupy. Place almonds on an oven tray lined with aluminium foil, pour syrup over and set aside until hard. Break into pieces, place in food processor and process to make coarse crumbs. Stir praline and Calvados into mascarpone or cream cheese.

4   To make Toffee Sauce, combine cream, butter and brown sugar in a saucepan. Stir over a low heat until smooth. Set aside to keep warm.

5   To assemble stacks, place a pastry square on each serving plate, top with half the apple slices and half the Mascarpone Praline Filling. Repeat with remaining pastry squares and apple slices and filling, ending with a third layer of pastry. Top with toffee sauce and serve immediately.

Chocolate Fans, Berry and Rose Petal Tuiles, Apple and Mascarpone Stacks

---

EDIBLE FLOWERS

There are a number of flowers that are quite safe to eat and can be used to add colour to desserts, salads and many other dishes. Some of the most common ones are roses, marigolds, zucchini, chrysanthemum, nasturtium and herb flowers such as borage, lavender and sage. But remember that some flowers are poisonous. If you are unsure always check before using them with food.

CHOCOLATE FANS

Serves 4

CHOCOLATE ROUNDS
- ☐ **125 g (4 oz) white chocolate, melted**
- ☐ **125 g (4 oz) milk chocolate, melted**
- ☐ **250 g (8 oz) dark chocolate, melted**

MOCHA CREAM
- ☐ **185 g (6 oz) dark chocolate**
- ☐ **4 tablespoons double cream**
- ☐ **3 tablespoons Tia Maria**
- ☐ **30 g (1 oz) butter**

PRALINE CREAM
- ☐ **125 g (4 oz) sugar**
- ☐ **3 tablespoons water**

China Limoges *Silverware* Oneida

BERRY AND ROSE PETAL TUILES

These thin French biscuits shaped into baskets and filled with fresh berries make a sophisticated and elegant dessert for a special occasion.

Serves 6
Oven temperature 180°C, 350°F, Gas 4

TUILES
- ☐ **3 tablespoons plain flour**
- ☐ **60 g (2 oz) butter, melted**
- ☐ **3 tablespoons caster sugar**
- ☐ **3 tablespoons ground almonds**
- ☐ **2 egg whites**
- ☐ **2 teaspoons rosewater**

BERRY FILLING
- ☐ **500 g (1 lb) mixed berries, such as strawberries, raspberries and blackberries**
- ☐ **3 miniature roses, petals removed**

ROSE CREAM
- ☐ **1 teaspoon rosewater**
- ☐ **pink food colouring**
- ☐ **155 mL (5 fl oz) double cream, whipped**

1   To make tuiles, combine flour, butter, sugar, ground almonds, egg whites and rosewater in a bowl and refrigerate for 20 minutes. Trim white base from rose petals, wash and pat dry.
2   Mark two 13 cm (5 in) circles on a greased and floured baking tray. Place a tablespoon of tuile mixture in each circle and spread out thinly to fill circles. Bake for 10-12 minutes.
3   Remove trays from oven and carefully lift biscuits from trays using a spatula. Press biscuits over base of a greased, small, flat-bottomed bowl to form a basket. Set aside to cool. Repeat with tuile mixture to make six baskets.
4   Fill cooled baskets with mixed berries and rose petals.
5   To make cream, fold rosewater and a few drops of food colouring into cream. Serve with filled tuiles.

- ☐ **3 tablespoons blanched almonds, toasted**
- ☐ **155 mL (5 fl oz) double cream, whipped**

1   To make Chocolate Rounds, line four baking trays with baking paper. Spread white chocolate on one tray and milk chocolate on another. Spread half the dark chocolate on each of the remaining trays. Spread out chocolate, using a spatula, to form 25 x 15 cm (10 x 6 in) rectangles. Set aside to firm at room temperature. Cut four 7.5 cm (3 in) circles from each rectangle of chocolate, using a pastry cutter.
2   To make Mocha Cream, place chocolate, cream, Tia Maria and butter in a saucepan and cook over a low heat until mixture is smooth. Remove from heat and cool for 5 minutes then beat until creamy.
3   To make Praline Cream, place sugar and water in a small saucepan, cook over a low heat, stirring until sugar dissolves. Increase heat and simmer sugar syrup until golden. Place almonds on a baking tray, pour syrup over and set aside until toffee hardens. Break almond toffee into pieces and place in a food processor and process to make small crumbs. Fold praline into whipped cream.
4   To assemble, place a dark chocolate round on each serving plate. Using half the Mocha Cream spread each round with it, then top with a milk chocolate round and spread with Praline Cream. Top with a white chocolate round and spread with remaining Mocha Cream. Finally top with remaining dark chocolate rounds and press each stack gently to fan out.

FOOD WITH SPIRIT

A dash of liqueur, or a splash of champagne, add that special touch to a dish. These recipes use a little alcohol to add that feeling of indulgence. Remember when using alcohol in cooking that more does not necessarily mean better.

LOBSTER PASTRIES WITH CHAMPAGNE SAUCE

Fresh asparagus, lobster and champagne – the ultimate indulgence.

Serves 6
Oven temperature 200°C, 400°F, Gas 6

- ☐ **170 g (5¹/₂ oz) prepared or ready-rolled puff pastry, thawed**
- ☐ **1 tablespoon water**
- ☐ **15 g (¹/₂ oz) flaked almonds**

CHAMPAGNE SAUCE
- ☐ **250 mL (8 fl oz) chicken stock**
- ☐ **125 mL (4 fl oz) champagne**
- ☐ **2 teaspoons grated lemon rind**
- ☐ **250 mL (8 fl oz) cream**
- ☐ **1 egg yolk, lightly beaten**
- ☐ **30 g (1 oz) butter mixed with 2 tablespoons plain flour**
- ☐ **1 teaspoon finely chopped fresh coriander**
- ☐ **freshly ground black pepper**

FILLING
- ☐ **250 g (8 oz) fresh asparagus, trimmed and cut into 7.5 cm (3 in) lengths**
- ☐ **2 uncooked lobster tails**
- ☐ **3 sprigs fresh coriander**
- ☐ **bouquet garni**
- ☐ **1 teaspoon whole green peppercorns**
- ☐ **100 g (3¹/₂ oz) watercress**

1   Cut pastry into six 10 x 5 cm (4 x 2 in) rectangles and place on a greased baking tray. Brush lightly with water and sprinkle with almonds. Bake for 15 minutes, or until pastry is golden brown and crisp. Set aside to cool on wire rack. Cut each rectangle into three horizontal layers.

2   To make Champagne Sauce, place stock, champagne and lemon rind in a small saucepan. Bring to the boil and boil until liquid is reduced by half. Strain and return to a clean pan. Combine cream and egg yolk and whisk into liquid. Whisk in butter mixture and cook over a low heat, without boiling, stirring constantly, until sauce thickens slightly. Stir coriander into sauce and season to taste with black pepper. Set aside and keep warm.

3   To make filling, boil, steam or microwave asparagus until tender. Refresh under cold running water. Drain and set aside. Place lobster tails, coriander, bouquet garni and peppercorns in a saucepan. Cover with water and simmer for 10-15 minutes or until cooked. Remove lobster tails from water and set aside to cool for 10 minutes. Shell tails and cut into thin medallions.

4   To serve, warm pastry rectangles in a low oven for 5 minutes. Place bottom layers on six serving plates. Top with half the asparagus and half the lobster and a few sprigs of watercress. Spoon sauce over. Repeat with remaining pastry, asparagus, lobster, watercress and sauce, finishing with almond pastry layer.

Lobster Pastries with Champagne Sauce

China Wedgewood *Lamp Inini*

17

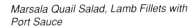

LAMB FILLETS WITH PORT SAUCE

Fillets of lamb, leeks and a port sauce make up this easy-to-prepare dish. Served with new potatoes and a salad of mixed lettuces and fresh herbs, you have a wonderfully indulgent meal.

Serves 6

- ☐ **3 tablespoons sugar**
- ☐ **3 tablespoons red wine vinegar**
- ☐ **375 mL (12 fl oz) beef stock**
- ☐ **140 g (4¹/₂ oz) butter**
- ☐ **6 leeks, cut into 5 mm (¹/₄ in) slices**
- ☐ **3 tablespoons water**
- ☐ **2 tablespoons oil**
- ☐ **3 lamb fillets, approximately 375 g (12 oz) each, trimmed of all visible fat and skin removed**
- ☐ **4 tablespoons port**
- ☐ **freshly ground black pepper**

1   Place sugar and vinegar in a small saucepan and cook over a low heat until sugar dissolves. Bring to the boil and boil until mixture caramelises. Stir in stock and simmer for 10 minutes. Set aside.
2   Melt 100 g (3¹/₂ oz) butter in a heavy-based frying pan, add leek slices and water and cook gently for 8 minutes, or until leeks are just tender. Set aside and keep warm.
3   Heat remaining butter and oil in a large heavy-based frying pan. When sizzling, add lamb fillets and cook for 5-7 minutes each side, or until browned. Remove from pan and set aside to keep warm. Place pan over a medium heat, add port and cook, scraping up caramelised juices in pan. Stir in reserved stock mixture and cook over a medium heat until sauce reduces and thickens. Season to taste with black pepper.
4   Divide leeks between six serving plates. Slice each lamb fillet into medallions and arrange on top of leeks. Spoon sauce over and serve immediately.

China Wedgwood *Silverware* Oneida

MARSALA QUAIL SALAD

In this salad the quail and marsala, with their distinctive flavours, mingle deliciously with the salad leaves. An elegant dish that can be served as a luncheon dish or starter.

Serves 6
Oven temperature 180°C, 350°F, Gas 4

- ☐ **6 quails**
- ☐ **30 g (1 oz) butter**
- ☐ **125 mL (4 fl oz) double cream**
- ☐ **185 mL (6 fl oz) dry Marsala**
- ☐ **1 curly endive, leaves separated**
- ☐ **1 chicory, leaves separated**
- ☐ **1 radicchio, leaves separated**
- ☐ **200 g (6¹/₂ oz) watercress**
- ☐ **1 pear, peeled, cored and sliced**
- ☐ **45 g (1¹/₂ oz) pecan nuts**

MARSALA SAUCE
- ☐ **125 mL (4 fl oz) double cream**
- ☐ **2 tablespoons mayonnaise**
- ☐ **2 teaspoons dry Marsala**

1   Place quails on a rack in a baking pan and bake for 20 minutes. Cool slightly, then break into serving-size portions.
2   Melt butter in a saucepan. Add cream and Marsala, bring to the boil, then reduce heat and simmer for 5 minutes. Add quail and cook for 5 minutes longer. Set aside to cool.
3   To make sauce, combine cream, mayonnaise and Marsala and beat well to combine.
4   Arrange endive, chicory, radicchio, watercress and pear in a serving bowl. Top with quail, sprinkle with pecan nuts and drizzle sauce over. Serve immediately.

FIG AND APPLE SOUFFLE

This light-as-air soufflé, fragrant with brandy and figs, is a delicious way to end any meal.

Serves 8
Oven temperature 180°C, 350° F, Gas 4

- ☐ **155 g (5 oz) dried figs, chopped**
- ☐ **2 tablespoons Calvados (apple brandy)**
- ☐ **140 g (4½ oz) apple purée**
- ☐ **3 tablespoons caster sugar**
- ☐ **4 egg whites**

1   Place figs and Calvados in a bowl and toss to combine. Set aside to marinate for 2 hours.
2   Combine apple purée, sugar, and fig mixture in a mixing bowl and stir until sugar dissolves.

3   Lightly grease an 18 cm (7 in) soufflé dish and sprinkle with a little caster sugar. Beat egg whites until stiff peaks form. Fold egg whites into apple mixture and spoon into prepared soufflé dish. Stand soufflé dish in a baking dish and pour in enough boiling water to come halfway up sides of dish. Bake for 20-25 minutes, or until well risen and firm to touch.

Fig and Apple Soufflé

❦

BEEF WRAPPED IN PASTRY WITH RED WINE SAUCE

Succulent beef surrounded by mushrooms and wrapped in puff pastry, this dish is sure to impress – this Master Class shows you how easy it is.

Serves 6
Oven temperature 220°C, 425°F, Gas 7

- ☐ **60 g (2 oz) butter**
- ☐ **1 kg (2 lb) fillet of beef in one piece, trimmed**
- ☐ **1 onion, chopped**
- ☐ **375 g (12 oz) button mushrooms, finely chopped**
- ☐ **freshly ground black pepper**
- ☐ **pinch ground nutmeg**
- ☐ **1 tablespoon finely chopped fresh parsley**
- ☐ **500 g (1 lb) prepared or ready-rolled puff pastry**
- ☐ **1 egg, lightly beaten**

RED WINE SAUCE
- ☐ **250 mL (8 fl oz) dry red wine**
- ☐ **1 teaspoon finely chopped fresh thyme, or ¹/₄ teaspoon dried thyme**
- ☐ **1 teaspoon finely chopped fresh parsley**
- ☐ **freshly ground black pepper**
- ☐ **100 g (3¹/₂ oz) butter, cut into eight pieces**
- ☐ **2 teaspoons cornflour, blended with 1 tablespoon water**

1 Melt half the butter in a heavy-based frying pan. When sizzling, add beef and cook over a medium heat for 10 minutes, turning to brown and seal on all sides. Remove pan from heat and set aside to cool completely.

2 Melt remaining butter in frying pan and cook onion for 5 minutes, or until soft. Add mushrooms and cook over a medium heat for 15 minutes, or until all the pan juices evaporate. Stir during cooking to prevent them sticking. Season to taste with black pepper and nutmeg, stir in parsley and set aside to cool completely.

3 Roll out pastry to 7.5 cm (3 in) longer than meat and wide enough to wrap around fillet. Spread half mushroom mixture down centre of pastry and place fillet on top. Spread remaining mushroom mixture on top of fillet. Cut corners out of pastry. Brush pastry edges with egg. Wrap pastry around fillet like a parcel, tucking ends in.

Turn pastry-wrapped fillet over and place on a lightly greased baking tray and freeze for 10 minutes.

4 Roll out pastry trimmings to a 30 x 10 cm (12 x 4 in) length and cut into strips 1 cm (¹/₂ in) wide. Remove fillet from freezer and brush pastry all over with egg. Arrange 5 pastry strips diagonally over pastry parcel, then arrange remaining strips diagonally in opposite direction. Brush top of strips only with egg. Bake for 30 minutes for medium-rare beef. Place on a warmed serving platter and set aside

to rest in a warm place for 10 minutes.

5 To make sauce, place wine in a small saucepan and cook over a medium heat until reduced by half. Add thyme and parsley and season to taste with black pepper. Remove pan from heat and quickly whisk in 1 piece of butter at a time, ensuring that each piece of butter is completely whisked in and melted before adding next. Pour in cornflour mixture and stir over a medium heat until sauce thickens. Serve with sliced beef.

Roll out pastry to a length 7.5 cm (3 in) longer than meat and wide enough to wrap around fillet. Spread half mushroom mixture down centre of pastry, and remaining mixture on top of fillet.

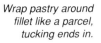

Wrap pastry around fillet like a parcel, tucking ends in.

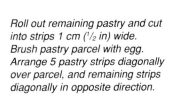

Roll out remaining pastry and cut into strips 1 cm (¹/₂ in) wide. Brush pastry parcel with egg. Arrange 5 pastry strips diagonally over parcel, and remaining strips diagonally in opposite direction.

China Noritake

OYSTER MOUSSELINE WITH CHAMPAGNE SAUCE

Just right as a starter for a summer dinner party. These delicious mousselines have a subtle flavour and are perfectly complemented by the accompanying Champagne Sauce.

Serves 6
Oven temperature 180°C, 350°F, Gas 4

- [ ] **36 prepared oysters**
- [ ] **60 g (2 oz) scallops**
- [ ] **60 g (2 oz) plaice or sole fillets, skinned**
- [ ] **2 egg whites**
- [ ] **1 egg yolk**
- [ ] **4 tablespoons cream**
- [ ] **freshly ground black pepper**
- [ ] **12 lollo rosso lettuce leaves, blanched**

CHAMPAGNE SAUCE
- [ ] **125 mL (4 fl oz) champagne**
- [ ] **4 tablespoons double cream**
- [ ] **200 g (6¹/₂ oz) unsalted butter, cut into pieces**

1   Place oysters, scallops and plaice or sole fillets in a food processor or blender and process until smooth. Push through a sieve. Place oyster mixture in a stainless steel bowl over ice. Beat egg whites until soft peaks form and set aside. Whisk egg yolk into cream a little at a time, then lightly fold in egg whites. Season to taste with black pepper.
2   Line six lightly greased, individual ramekins with lettuce leaves, allowing leaves to overhang top. Divide fish mixture evenly between ramekins and fold leaves over.
3   Cover each ramekin with foil. Place ramekins in a baking dish and pour in enough hot water to come halfway up sides of ramekins. Bake for 35-40 minutes, or until a skewer inserted in the centre comes out clean. Set aside for 5 minutes before turning out.
4   To make sauce, place champagne in a saucepan, bring to the boil and cook until reduced by half. Stir in cream and simmer until sauce is reduced and of a creamy consistency. Gradually whisk in butter a piece at a time. Whisk well after each addition. Serve with mousseline.

ORANGE LIQUEUR BABAS

An adaptation of the traditional rum baba, this recipe uses Grand Marnier in place of rum. It is said that the original rum baba came about when the Polish king Stanislas Leszcsunski was exiled to Lorraine. He found the kugelhopf too dry and so poured rum over it, then named it after his favourite hero, Ali Baba.

Serves 6
Oven temperature 200°C, 400°F, Gas 6

- [ ] **125 g (4 oz) plain flour, sifted**
- [ ] **1¹/₂ teaspoons dry yeast**
- [ ] **1 teaspoon sugar**
- [ ] **60 g (2 oz) butter, melted**
- [ ] **2 eggs, lightly beaten**
- [ ] **4 tablespoons milk, warmed**
- [ ] **2 tablespoons finely chopped dried pears**
- [ ] **2 tablespoons finely chopped dried apricots**

ORANGE SYRUP
- [ ] **125 mL (4 fl oz) water**
- [ ] **3 tablespoons sugar**
- [ ] **2 tablespoons orange juice**
- [ ] **2 tablespoons Grand Marnier (orange liqueur)**

APRICOT GLAZE
- [ ] **2 tablespoons sieved apricot jam, warmed with 1¹/₂ tablespoons water**
- [ ] **crystallised orange rind**

1   Combine flour, yeast and sugar in a mixing bowl. Whisk butter, eggs and milk together and beat into flour mixture. Continue to beat for 3-4 minutes.
2   Stir pears and apricots into batter. Spoon batter into six, greased individual baba moulds – the mixture should only one-third fill the moulds. Cover each mould with plastic food wrap and set aside in a warm place to rise for 30 minutes, or until mixture doubles in size. Bake for 15-20 minutes, or until golden and cooked through. Remove from oven and set aside to cool in moulds.
3   To make Orange Syrup, place water and sugar in a small saucepan and cook over a low heat, stirring constantly, until sugar dissolves. Bring to the boil and simmer for 5 minutes, without stirring. Remove from heat and stir in orange juice and Grand Marnier. Prick cooled babas with a skewer and pour hot syrup over. Set aside to cool.
4   Turn babas out and brush with apricot glaze. Decorate with crystallised orange rind.

MARINATED PORK SPARE RIBS

American pork spare ribs are a barbecue favourite. In this recipe they are marinated in wine with rosemary and fennel seeds and glazed with wine and mustard to make an extra-special dish.

Serves 4
Oven temperature 200°C, 400°F, Gas 6

- [ ] **4 racks pork spare ribs, each with 6 ribs**
- [ ] **2 tablespoons vegetable oil**

MARINADE
- [ ] **1¹/₂ tablespoons rock salt**
- [ ] **125 g (4 oz) sugar**
- [ ] **6 sprigs fresh rosemary, chopped**
- [ ] **3 tablespoons fennel seeds**
- [ ] **coarsely grated rind 2 oranges**
- [ ] **250 mL (8 fl oz) white wine**

WINE AND MUSTARD SAUCE
- [ ] **3 tablespoons white wine**
- [ ] **2 tablespoons wholegrain mustard**
- [ ] **2 tablespoons redcurrant jelly**

1   To make marinade, combine rock salt, sugar, rosemary, fennel seeds, orange rind and wine in a large shallow dish. Cut ribs into groups of two. Add ribs and turn to coat well, cover and refrigerate overnight. Turn occasionally.
2   Heat oil in a large baking pan. Remove ribs from marinade and place in baking pan, cook for 15-20 minutes, basting occasionally with marinade. Remove ribs from tin and set aside to keep warm.
3   To make sauce, pour excess oil from pan, place tin over a high heat, add wine and cook, scraping up caramelised juices in pan. Stir in mustard and jelly and mix well to combine. Continue to cook until sauce is thick and syrupy. Just prior to serving, return ribs to pan and toss in sauce to coat.

Marinated Pork Spare Ribs, Oyster Mousseline with Champagne Sauce, Orange Liqueur Babas

SUPER SAUCES

Hollandaise Sauce turns salmon into a really special treat. Fresh homemade pesto makes pasta a luxury and veloute is the base for many of the best sauces. With this selection of sauces you can add that special touch to a meal in next to no time.

From top: Pesto Sauce, Indulgent Mayonnaise, Creamy Broccoli Sauce, Hollandaise Sauce, Rich Tomato Sauce, White Wine Vinaigrette

CREAMY BROCCOLI SAUCE

Serve this sauce as soon as it is made. It is delicious tossed through cooked pasta or served with chicken or fish.

Makes 750 mL (1¼ pt)

- ☐ **1 head broccoli, broken into small florets**
- ☐ **60 g (2 oz) butter**
- ☐ **2 teaspoons wholegrain mustard**
- ☐ **6 spring onions, finely chopped**
- ☐ **3 tablespoons plain flour**
- ☐ **440 mL (14 fl oz) chicken stock**
- ☐ **3 tablespoons white wine**
- ☐ **125 mL (4 fl oz) cream**
- ☐ **1½ teaspoons grated lemon rind**
- ☐ **freshly ground black pepper**

1 Boil, steam or microwave broccoli until tender. Drain and refresh under cold running water. Drain and set aside.
2 Melt butter in a saucepan, then add mustard and spring onions and cook over a medium heat for 2-3 minutes. Stir in flour and cook for 1 minute longer. Gradually stir in stock and wine and cook, stirring constantly, until sauce boils and thickens.
3 Remove pan from heat and blend in cream, lemon rind, and black pepper to taste. Place broccoli in a food processor or blender and process until smooth. Stir broccoli into sauce and heat gently.

RICH TOMATO SAUCE

Serve this sauce with any boiled, steamed or microwaved vegetables. Top with breadcrumbs and Parmesan cheese and place under a hot grill to create a tomato-flavoured gratin.

Makes 500 mL (16 fl oz)

- ☐ **2 tablespoons olive oil**
- ☐ **2 leeks, white part finely sliced**
- ☐ **440 g (14 oz) canned tomato purée**
- ☐ **2 x 440 g (14 oz) canned peeled tomatoes, undrained and chopped**
- ☐ **2 teaspoons finely chopped fresh rosemary**
- ☐ **1 tablespoon finely chopped fresh basil**
- ☐ **2 cloves garlic, crushed**
- ☐ **250 mL (8 fl oz) canned beef consommé**
- ☐ **½ teaspoon sugar**
- ☐ **freshly ground black pepper**

1 Heat oil in a heavy-based saucepan and cook leeks over a medium heat for 4-5 minutes, or until soft.
2 Stir in tomato purée, tomatoes, rosemary, basil, garlic, beef consommé, sugar, and black pepper to taste. Cook over a low heat, stirring frequently, for 1 hour or until sauce thickens.

WHITE WINE VINAIGRETTE

It is easy to alter the flavour of this vinaigrette by using different oils and different vinegars. You might like to try walnut or hazelnut oil, or a red wine or cider vinegar.

Makes 250 mL (8 fl oz)

- ☐ **4 tablespoons olive oil**
- ☐ **4 tablespoons groundnut oil**
- ☐ **3 tablespoons white wine vinegar**
- ☐ **1 tablespoon French mustard**
- ☐ **freshly ground black pepper**

Place olive oil, groundnut oil, vinegar, mustard and black pepper to taste in a screwtop jar. Shake well to combine all ingredients.

Variations

Lemon Herb Vinaigrette: Replace vinegar with 3 tablespoons lemon juice, and add 4 tablespoons mixed chopped fresh herbs. Suggested herbs include basil, parsley, chives, rosemary, thyme or tarragon.

Hazelnut Vinaigrette: Replace olive oil with 4 tablespoons hazelnut oil and groundnut oil with 4 tablespoons polyunsaturated oil, such as sunflower or safflower oil. You can also add finely chopped hazelnuts just before serving.

VELOUTE

The base of the Creamy Broccoli Sauce is a velouté sauce. This sauce forms the base of many of the best sauces.

❧ A velouté sauce is a white sauce that uses milk or stock, or a combination of the two, as the liquid.
❧ The flavour and colour can be changed by using different vegetable purées and stocks.
❧ Omitting the vegetable purée and mustard gives a true velouté sauce that will stand on its own as an accompaniment to eggs, fish, poultry veal and vegetables.
❧ When making the sauce to go with fish use fish stock.

Above: Rich Tomato Sauce
Right: Pesto Sauce

INDULGENT MAYONNAISE

Thick, creamy homemade mayonnaise is easy to make using a food processor and adds a touch of indulgence to any salad.

Makes 500 g (8 oz)

- ☐ **6 egg yolks**
- ☐ **1 teaspoon French mustard**
- ☐ **1 tablespoon lemon or lime juice**
- ☐ **1 tablespoon tarragon vinegar**
- ☐ **250 mL (8 fl oz) grapeseed oil**
- ☐ **250 mL (8 fl oz) groundnut oil**
- ☐ **freshly ground black pepper**
- ☐ **1 tablespoon boiling water**

1 Place egg yolks, mustard, lemon or lime juice and vinegar in a food processor or blender and process until well mixed. Combine grapeseed oil and groundnut oil. With machine running, slowly pour in oil mixture and process until mixture thickens.
2 Season to taste with black pepper and stir in water. Transfer to a jar, cover and refrigerate for up to 3 weeks.

Variations

Garlic Mayonnaise: Add 6 cloves peeled garlic to the egg yolk mixture and replace lemon or lime juice and tarragon vinegar with 2 tablespoons lemon juice.
Green Herbed Mayonnaise: Replace lemon or lime juice and tarragon vinegar with 2 tablespoons cider vinegar. Purée 30 g (1 oz) fresh basil leaves, 2 tablespoons fresh parsley, 12 fresh chives and 1 clove garlic. Stir into prepared mayonnaise.

PESTO SAUCE

This traditional Italian sauce with its garlic and basil flavour is marvellous to have on hand to pep up vegetable soups, sauces, or just to toss through hot vegetables or pasta. Pesto can be stored in the refrigerator for up to two weeks.

Makes 315 mL (10 fl oz)

- ☐ **60 g (2 oz) fresh basil leaves**
- ☐ **4 cloves garlic, crushed**
- ☐ **4 tablespoons pine nuts, toasted**
- ☐ **60 g (2 oz) grated fresh Parmesan cheese**
- ☐ **155 mL (5 fl oz) olive oil**

Place basil, garlic and pine nuts in a food processor or blender and process until combined. Add cheese and oil and process until smooth.

HOLLANDAISE SAUCE

The secret to success when making this sauce is to have the temperature right; it should be hot enough to thicken the sauce but not so hot that it will curdle. To achieve this, set the bowl over simmering water during cooking.

Makes 250 mL (8 fl oz)

- ☐ **3¹/₂ tablespoons white vinegar**
- ☐ **1¹/₂ tablespoons water**
- ☐ **12 whole peppercorns**
- ☐ **1 bay leaf**
- ☐ **3 egg yolks**
- ☐ **200 g (6¹/₂ oz) butter, softened**
- ☐ **freshly ground black pepper**

1 Place vinegar, water, peppercorns and bay leaf in a saucepan. Bring to the boil and boil until mixture reduces to a third. Remove from heat and set aside to cool.
2 Place egg yolks in a heatproof bowl and whisk with 30 g (1 oz) butter. Strain vinegar mixture and whisk into egg mixture. Place bowl over a saucepan of simmering water and whisk constantly until mixture thickens.
3 Remove saucepan from heat and whisk in remaining butter, a little at a time, until sauce is thick, shiny and resembles a thick cream. Season to taste with black pepper and serve immediately.

Variation

Bearnaise Sauce: Add 3 finely chopped spring onions to vinegar mixture, replace white vinegar with tarragon vinegar and make in the same way as for Hollandaise Sauce.

SEAFOOD SPECTACULAR

As a light main course or starter for a dinner party, seafood is a popular indulgence. These recipes use easy techniques to retain the wonderful flavours, but have an added twist to place them in the realm of super indulgences.

SALAD OF LOBSTER WITH RASPBERRIES

Lobster is the undisputed king of shellfish. In this recipe, it is taken to new heights with the addition of a raspberry dressing.

Serves 4

- ☐ **2 lobster tails, cooked and shells removed**
- ☐ **1 small radicchio, leaves separated**
- ☐ **1 small lollo rosso lettuce, leaves separated**
- ☐ **100 g (3¹/₂ oz) watercress**
- ☐ **1 orange, segmented**
- ☐ **250 g (8 oz) strawberries, halved**

DRESSING
- ☐ **125 g (4 oz) fresh or frozen raspberries**
- ☐ **2 tablespoons raspberry vinegar**
- ☐ **2 tablespoons vegetable oil**
- ☐ **1 teaspoon finely chopped fresh mint**
- ☐ **1 tablespoon sugar**

1   Cut lobster tails into 1 cm (¹/₂ in) medallions and set aside.
2   Arrange radicchio, lettuce, watercress, lobster, orange segments and strawberries attractively on a serving platter and refrigerate until required.
3   To make dressing, place raspberries in a food processor or blender and process until puréed. Push through a sieve to remove seeds. Combine raspberry purée with vinegar, oil, mint and sugar. Mix well to combine, pour over salad and serve immediately.

Salad of Lobster with Raspberries

MUSSEL AND VEGETABLE FLANS

Serves 4
Oven temperature 220°C, 425°F, Gas 7

PASTRY
- [ ] 185 g (6 oz) plain flour, sifted
- [ ] 1/4 teaspoon baking powder
- [ ] 125 g (4 oz) butter, cubed and chilled
- [ ] 1 egg yolk
- [ ] 1-2 tablespoons iced water
- [ ] 1/2 teaspoon lemon juice

FILLING
- [ ] 16 mussels, scrubbed and bearded
- [ ] 1 leek, cut into thin strips
- [ ] 2 large carrots, cut into thin strips
- [ ] 1 tablespoon finely chopped fresh coriander
- [ ] 315 mL (10 fl oz) double cream
- [ ] 12 uncooked prawns, peeled and deveined
- [ ] 1 1/2 tablespoons plain flour

China Incorporated Agencies

LIME BATTERED SEAFOOD WITH MAYONNAISE

Never before have fish and chips been this good. Make your own chips and no one will be able to resist.

Serves 4

- [ ] 8 large uncooked prawns, peeled, tails attached and deveined
- [ ] 2 squid hoods, cleaned and cut into rings
- [ ] 4 thick white fish fillets, such as whiting
- [ ] oil for deep-frying

BATTER
- [ ] 185 g (6 oz) plain flour, sifted
- [ ] 125 mL (4 fl oz) lime juice
- [ ] 250 mL (8 fl oz) soda water
- [ ] 2 teaspoons finely grated lime rind

MAYONNAISE
- [ ] 3 egg yolks
- [ ] 1/4 teaspoon dry mustard
- [ ] 250 mL (8 fl oz) vegetable oil
- [ ] 2 tablespoons lemon juice
- [ ] 1 tablespoon finely chopped fresh coriander
- [ ] freshly ground black pepper

1   To make batter, place flour in a bowl and gradually stir in lime juice and soda water. Mix well to combine, then stir in lime rind. Set aside.

2   To make mayonnaise, place egg yolks and mustard in a food processor or blender and, with machine running, slowly pour in oil and process until mixture thickens. Blend in lemon juice. Stir in coriander and season to taste with black pepper.

3   Heat oil to 180°C (350°) in a large saucepan. Dip prawns, squid and fish in batter, drain off excess and deep-fry a few at a time in hot oil, until golden. Remove from pan and drain on absorbent kitchen paper. Serve with mayonnaise.

Above: Lime Battered Seafood with Mayonnaise

- ☐ **30 g (1 oz) butter, softened**
- ☐ **freshly ground black pepper**

1 To make pastry, place flour, baking powder and butter in a food processor or blender and process until mixture resembles coarse breadcrumbs. Combine egg yolk, water and lemon juice and, with machine running, gradually pour in egg mixture, until a soft dough forms. Wrap in plastic food wrap. Refrigerate for 1 hour.

2 Divide pastry into four portions and roll out thinly on a lightly floured surface. Line four 12 cm (5 in) flan tins with pastry, prick base of flans with a fork. Line flans with baking paper and fill with beans. Bake for 5 minutes, remove paper and beans and bake for 12 minutes longer.

3 To make filling, place mussels in a large saucepan and add just enough water to cover mussels. Cook over a low heat until shells open. Discard unopened shells. Remove mussel meat and discard shells. Reserve 125 mL (4 fl oz) of pan liquid. Heat reserved liquid in a frying pan and cook leek, carrot and coriander for 2 minutes.

4 Stir in cream, mussels and prawns and cook over a low heat for 5 minutes. Mix flour and butter together to form a paste, then whisk in small pieces into cream mixture and cook for 2-3 minutes, or until thickened. Season to taste with black pepper. Spoon filling into warm pastry shells and serve.

MIXED SEAFOOD WITH PARSLEY CREAM

Serves 4

- ☐ **5 tablespoons olive oil**
- ☐ **3 cloves garlic, crushed**
- ☐ **100 g (3¹/₂ oz) red snapper or sea bass fillets, skinned and cut into 8 pieces**
- ☐ **100 g (3¹/₂ oz) salmon trout fillets, skinned and cut into 8 pieces**
- ☐ **12 large uncooked prawns, peeled and deveined**
- ☐ **8 scallops**

TOMATO SALAD
- ☐ **3 ripe tomatoes, peeled, seeded and diced**
- ☐ **1¹/₂ tablespoons chopped fresh coriander**
- ☐ **1 tablespoon olive oil**
- ☐ **freshly ground black pepper**

PARSLEY CREAM
- ☐ **5 tablespoons finely chopped fresh parsley**
- ☐ **3 tablespoons double cream**
- ☐ **3 tablespoons mayonnaise**

1 To make salad, place tomatoes, coriander, oil, and black pepper to taste in a bowl and toss to combine. Set aside.

2 To make cream, place parsley, cream and mayonnaise in a food processor or blender and process until smooth.

3 Heat oil in a frying pan and cook garlic, snapper, trout, prawns and scallops over a low heat for 6-7 minutes. Turn seafood gently during cooking, taking care not to damage whole pieces. Arrange seafood and Tomato Salad on four serving plates, spoon Parsley Cream over and serve.

Mussel and Vegetable Flans, Mixed Seafood with Parsley Cream

China Incorporated Agencies Silverware R.P. Symons

❧

SALMON MOSAIC WITH WINE SAUCE

Your guests will be hooked on this luxurious combination of salmon and spinach that is perfectly complemented by a creamy sauce.

Serves 4

- ☐ **4 large white fish fillets, such as cod**
- ☐ **2 tablespoons lemon juice**
- ☐ **freshly ground white pepper**
- ☐ **16 large spinach leaves, stalks removed and blanched**
- ☐ **2 salmon fillets, skinned**
- ☐ **4 square pieces aluminium foil, buttered**

SAUCE
- ☐ **45 g (1¹/₂ oz) unsalted butter**
- ☐ **2 tablespoons chopped spring onions**
- ☐ **1 clove garlic, chopped**
- ☐ **2 fresh sage leaves**
- ☐ **200 g (6¹/₂ oz) young sorrel or spinach leaves**
- ☐ **500 mL (16 fl oz) fish stock**
- ☐ **1 bay leaf**
- ☐ **125 mL (4 fl oz) dry white wine**
- ☐ **250 mL (8 fl oz) double cream**
- ☐ **freshly ground black pepper**

1   Cut each cod fillet into four strips lengthways, each measuring 15 x 2.5 cm (6 x 1 in) – this will give you sixteen strips. Sprinkle with 1 tablespoon lemon juice and season to taste with white pepper. Wrap each strip in blanched spinach leaves.

2   Cut each salmon fillet into eight strips crossways to same size as cod strips. Sprinkle with remaining lemon juice and season to taste with white pepper.

3   Weave four strips of each fish into a square to form a chequerboard pattern on each piece of foil. Trim ends if necessary. Place a wire rack and 2.5 cm (1 in) of water in a large frying pan, cover and bring to the boil. Place fish parcels on wire rack and steam for 6-8 minutes, or until fish flakes when tested with a fork.

4   To make sauce, melt half the butter in a saucepan and cook spring onions, garlic and sage for 2 minutes. Add sorrel or spinach and cook over a low heat for 5 minutes, or until sorrel leaves are wilted. Add stock, bay leaf and wine. Bring to the boil and boil until mixture reduces by half. Remove bay leaf.

5   Place sauce in a food processor or blender and process until smooth. Pass through a fine sieve, then return to a clean saucepan. Stir in cream and cook over a low heat for 5 minutes. Whisk in small pieces of remaining butter. Season to taste with black pepper and set aside to keep warm. Serve fish squares with sauce.

Cut each cod fillet into four strips lengthways, sprinkle with lemon juice and season with white pepper. Wrap each strip in blanched spinach leaves.

Weave four strips of each fish into a square to form a chequerboard pattern on each piece of foil.

China Villeroy & Boch

FRESH HERB AND TOMATO SEAFOOD SOUP

A combination of fresh seafood and herbs helps to make this soup the perfect one-pot meal.

Serves 6

- ☐ 3 tablespoons olive oil
- ☐ 1 large red onion, thinly sliced
- ☐ 2 cloves garlic, crushed
- ☐ 2 litres (3½ pt) fish stock
- ☐ 440 g (14 oz) canned tomatoes, undrained and mashed
- ☐ 3 tablespoons white wine
- ☐ ¼ teaspoon ground saffron
- ☐ ¼ teaspoon Tabasco sauce
- ☐ 1 teaspoon sugar
- ☐ freshly ground black pepper
- ☐ 500 g (1 lb) thick white fish fillets, such as cod or monkfish, skinned and cut into 2.5 cm (1 in) cubes
- ☐ 60 g (2 oz) grated fresh Parmesan cheese
- ☐ 3 egg yolks, lightly beaten with 1 tablespoon water
- ☐ 1 tablespoon finely chopped fresh basil
- ☐ 1 teaspoon finely chopped fresh lemon thyme
- ☐ 12 mussels, scrubbed and bearded
- ☐ 6 baby octopuses or squid, heads removed and bodies and leg sections cut into quarters
- ☐ 12 large uncooked prawns, peeled and deveined
- ☐ 2 large uncooked crabs, claws and legs removed and bodies halved
- ☐ 1 tablespoon finely chopped fresh parsley

1   Heat oil in a large saucepan and cook onion and garlic for 2 minutes. Add fish stock, tomatoes, wine, saffron, Tabasco, sugar, and black pepper to taste and cook over a low heat for 10 minutes.

2   Add fish and half the Parmesan cheese. Gradually whisk in egg yolk mixture and stir gently until combined.

3   Add basil, thyme, mussels, octopus or squid, prawns and crab to soup, and cook over a low heat for 5 minutes. Remove any mussels which remain unopened. Serve garnished with parsley and remaining Parmesan cheese.

ASPARAGUS-FILLED FISH WITH PEPPERCORN SAUCE

Thick succulent fillets of fish, filled with scallops and asparagus and served with a creamy peppercorn sauce. This is a great do-ahead dish as the preparation of the fish fillets can be done earlier in the day.

Serves 6
Oven temperature 180°C, 350°F, Gas 4

- ☐ 6 thick white fish fillets, such as cod, haddock or monkfish, skinned
- ☐ 155 g (5 oz) scallops, chopped
- ☐ 6 fresh asparagus spears, cut into 2.5 cm (1 in) pieces and blanched
- ☐ 3 tablespoons sour cream
- ☐ 1 tablespoon snipped fresh chives
- ☐ freshly ground black pepper

GREEN PEPPERCORN SAUCE
- ☐ 375 mL (12 fl oz) double cream
- ☐ 2 tablespoons green peppercorns in brine, drained
- ☐ 10 fresh basil leaves

1   Cut a pocket in the side of each fish fillet, taking care not to cut right through fillet.

2   Place scallops, asparagus, sour cream, chives, and black pepper to taste in a bowl and mix to combine. Spoon mixture into pockets of fillets and secure with toothpicks. Place fish in a lightly oiled baking tin and cook for 10-15 minutes, or until flesh flakes when tested.

3   To make sauce, place cream, peppercorns and basil leaves in a frying pan and cook over a low heat for 10-15 minutes, or until mixture thickens slightly. Remove basil from sauce. Remove toothpicks from fish, spoon sauce over and serve immediately.

Fresh Herb and Tomato Seafood Soup, Asparagus-Filled Fish with Peppercorn Sauce, Smoked Salmon and Fresh Fruit Salad

China Bohemia Crystal

SMOKED SALMON AND FRESH FRUIT SALAD

This salad is a summer meal in itself. Accompany with crusty bread or rolls and you have a completely indulgent meal.

Serves 6

- ☐ **1 small pawpaw, or 2 small mangoes, peeled, seeded and cut into thick slices and tossed in lemon juice**
- ☐ **2 ripe avocados, stoned, peeled and cut into thick slices**
- ☐ **45 g (1½ oz) watercress**
- ☐ **24 slices smoked salmon**

DRESSING
- ☐ **2 tablespoons olive oil**
- ☐ **3 tablespoons lime juice**
- ☐ **125 mL (4 fl oz) orange juice**
- ☐ **pulp of 3 passion fruit**
- ☐ **2 tablespoons sugar**
- ☐ **freshly ground black pepper**

1   Arrange pawpaw or mangoes, avocado, watercress and salmon attractively on six individual serving plates. Cover and chill lightly.

2   To make dressing, place oil, lime juice, orange juice, passion fruit pulp, sugar, and black pepper to taste in a screwtop jar. Shake well to combine. Just prior to serving pour dressing over salad.

FISHY TALES

❦ When buying fish freshness is vital. Look for fish with bright scales, firm flesh, bright clear eyes and moist, bright pink gills.

❦ Always purchase fish as close to cooking time as possible and from a fishmonger that has a good turnover.

❦ Any fish that smells is suspect. Do not buy or eat it as it is sure to lead to food poisoning.

BANQUET FOR TWELVE

Take advantage of summer sunshine and lay the table for this indulgent smorgasbord – alfresco style. Much of the menu can be prepared ahead of time leaving only the final cooking and assembly to the last minute.

MENU
Smoked Salmon and
Potato Rounds

Coriander Mussels with
Lime Mayonnaise

Layered Pork Roast

Chicken Kebabs with
Raspberry Hollandaise

Peach Salad with
Mango Dressing

Summer Fruit Tartlets

SMOKED SALMON AND POTATO ROUNDS

The potato rounds and the topping for these delicious morsels can be prepared ahead of time. However, leave the final assembly until just prior to serving.

Makes 24

- ☐ 2 potatoes, peeled, finely grated and squeezed of excess liquid
- ☐ 1 egg, lightly beaten
- ☐ freshly ground black pepper
- ☐ 60 g (2 oz) butter
- ☐ 100 g (3^1/$_2$ oz) smoked salmon, cut into 1 cm (^{1}/$_2$ in) strips
- ☐ 1 lime

HORSERADISH SAUCE
- ☐ 2 teaspoons white wine vinegar
- ☐ 1 tablespoon horseradish relish
- ☐ ^{1}/$_2$ teaspoon caster sugar
- ☐ freshly ground black pepper
- ☐ 125 mL (4 oz) double cream

1 Place potato and egg in a bowl and mix well to combine. Season to taste with black pepper. Shape mixture into 24 balls and flatten slightly to form 2.5 cm (1 in) rounds.
2 Melt 15 g (^{1}/$_2$ oz) butter in a frying pan and cook 6 potato rounds until golden brown on both sides and cooked through. Remove from pan and allow to cool on a wire rack. Repeat with remaining butter and mixture until all rounds are cooked.
3 To make Horseradish Sauce, combine vinegar, horseradish and sugar in a mixing bowl. Season to taste with black pepper. Beat cream until stiff peaks form. Fold through horseradish mixture.
4 Peel lime with a vegetable peeler and cut rind into fine strips. Spread each potato round with horseradish cream and top with strips of salmon and lime.

CORIANDER MUSSELS WITH LIME MAYONNAISE

These delicious fritters can be prepared earlier in the day and final cooking done just prior to serving. The mayonnaise can be made 2-3 days in advance.

Makes 24

- ☐ 24 mussels, cleaned and bearded
- ☐ 2 large bunches fresh coriander, leaves removed
- ☐ 4 tablespoons pine nuts
- ☐ 6 cloves garlic, crushed
- ☐ 4 tablespoons olive oil
- ☐ 4 tablespoons grated fresh Parmesan cheese
- ☐ 155 g (5 oz) breadcrumbs made from stale bread
- ☐ freshly ground black pepper
- ☐ 60 g (2 oz) plain flour
- ☐ 2 eggs, lightly beaten with 2 tablespoons milk

LIME MAYONNAISE
- ☐ 3 egg yolks
- ☐ 250 mL (8 fl oz) oil
- ☐ 2 tablespoons lime juice
- ☐ freshly ground black pepper

1 Cook mussels in a large saucepan of boiling water for 2-3 minutes, or until shells open. Remove mussels from water as they open to avoid overcooking. Discard any mussels that have not opened after 5 minutes cooking. Remove mussel meat from shells, drain on absorbent kitchen paper and set aside.
2 Place coriander leaves, pine nuts, garlic and 1 tablespoon oil in a food processor or blender and process until combined. With machine running, slowly add remaining oil. Transfer mixture to a bowl and mix in Parmesan cheese and breadcrumbs. Season to taste with black pepper.
3 Lightly dust mussel meat with flour, dip in egg mixture and roll in coriander mixture, pressing firmly to coat mussels. Refrigerate for 30 minutes.
4 Place under preheated grill and cook on both sides until pesto is golden.
5 To make mayonnaise, place egg yolks in a food processor or blender and with machine running, slowly pour in oil. Process until well combined and mixture thickens. Add lime juice and season to taste with black pepper. Serve with hot mussels.

LAYERED PORK ROAST

Serves 12
Oven temperature 180°C, 350°F, Gas 4

- ☐ 3 pork tenderloins, approximately 375 g (12 oz) each, trimmed of excess fat
- ☐ 12 bacon rashers, rind removed
- ☐ 250 mL (8 fl oz) dry white wine

SPINACH STUFFING
- ☐ 30 g (1 oz) butter
- ☐ ^{1}/$_2$ onion, chopped
- ☐ 125 g (4 oz) button mushrooms, sliced
- ☐ 250 g (8 oz) spinach, stalks removed and leaves shredded
- ☐ ^{1}/$_2$ teaspoon ground nutmeg
- ☐ 30 g (1 oz) shelled pistachio nuts
- ☐ freshly ground black pepper

TOMATO STUFFING
- ☐ 30 g (1 oz) butter
- ☐ ^{1}/$_2$ onion, sliced
- ☐ 1 clove garlic, crushed
- ☐ 2 tomatoes, peeled, seeded and finely chopped
- ☐ ^{1}/$_2$ apple, peeled, cored and finely chopped
- ☐ 1 tablespoon tomato purée
- ☐ 1 teaspoon sugar
- ☐ pulp of 1 passion fruit
- ☐ 60 g (2 oz) breadcrumbs made from stale bread
- ☐ freshly ground black pepper

1 To make Spinach Stuffing, melt butter in a frying pan and cook onion for 4-5 minutes or until soft. Add mushrooms and cook for 4 minutes longer. Stir in spinach and cook until wilted. Remove from heat and mix in nutmeg and pistachio nuts. Season to taste with black pepper.
2 To make Tomato Stuffing, melt butter in a frying pan and cook onion and garlic for 4-5 minutes or until soft. Add tomatoes, apple, tomato purée, sugar and passion fruit pulp and cook for 3 minutes longer. Stir in breadcrumbs and season to taste with black pepper.
3 Slit each pork tenderloin lengthways, three-quarters of the way through. Open out each piece of meat so that it is as flat as possible. Top one piece with spinach mixture and place a second piece on top. Spread with tomato mixture and top with remaining tenderloin.
4 Wrap bacon rashers around meat and tie with string to secure roll. Place on a roasting rack in a baking tin and pour wine into dish. Bake 1^1/$_2$-2 hours, or until cooked through, basting frequently with juices in tin. Allow to cool completely.

CHICKEN KEBABS WITH RASPBERRY HOLLANDAISE

Succulent strips of chicken grilled and topped with a fruity hollandaise. If you are serving this meal outdoors, why not cook these kebabs on the barbecue.

Makes 12

- [ ] **6 boneless chicken breast fillets**

RASPBERRY MARINADE
- [ ] **125 mL (4 fl oz) olive oil**
- [ ] **1¹/₂ tablespoons raspberry vinegar**
- [ ] **2 teaspoons Framboise (raspberry liqueur)**
- [ ] **1 clove garlic, crushed**

RASPBERRY HOLLANDAISE SAUCE
- [ ] **3 egg yolks**
- [ ] **3 tablespoons water**
- [ ] **185 g (6 oz) butter, clarified and cooled to tepid**
- [ ] **125 g (4 oz) raspberries, puréed**
- [ ] **1 teaspoon raspberry vinegar**
- [ ] **1 tablespoon finely chopped fresh basil**
- [ ] **freshly ground black pepper**

1 To make marinade, combine oil, vinegar, liqueur and garlic in a screwtop jar and shake well to combine.
2 Cut chicken into thin strips and thread on to twelve oiled wooden skewers. Place into a shallow dish and pour marinade over. Cover and refrigerate for 2 hours or overnight.
3 To make sauce, whisk egg yolks and water in a bowl over a saucepan of simmering water, until mixture is light in colour. Cook over a low heat, whisking constantly until mixture becomes thick enough to leave a trail – take care not to overheat. Remove saucepan from heat and add butter a little at a time, whisking continuously until sauce thickens, then add remaining butter in a steady stream. Stir through raspberry purée, raspberry vinegar and basil. Season to taste with black pepper. Set aside and keep warm.
4 Cook kebabs under a preheated grill for 5-10 minutes, or until browned and cooked through, basting frequently with marinade. Serve with sauce.

PEACH SALAD WITH MANGO DRESSING

Lettuce and snow pea sprouts or watercress create the base for this colourful salad of summer fruits.

Serves 12

- [ ] **6 peaches, peeled and stoned**
- [ ] **freshly ground black pepper**
- [ ] **100 g (3¹/₂ oz) watercress**
- [ ] **2 butter lettuces, leaves separated and torn into pieces**
- [ ] **155 g (5 oz) macadamia or cashew nuts, roughly chopped**

MANGO DRESSING
- [ ] **1 large ripe mango, stoned, peeled and chopped**
- [ ] **2 tablespoons olive oil**
- [ ] **2 tablespoons white wine vinegar**
- [ ] **1 tablespoon snipped fresh chives**

1 To make dressing, place mango, oil and vinegar in a food processor or blender and process until smooth. Stir in chives.
2 Sprinkle peaches liberally with black pepper and arrange with watercress, lettuce and nuts on a serving platter. Pour dressing over.

SUMMER FRUIT TARTLETS

The perfect finish to the perfect meal. Use any fresh fruit of your choice in these delicately delicious tartlets.

Makes 12
Oven temperature 220°C, 425°F, Gas 7

- [ ] **185 g (6 oz) plain flour, sifted**
- [ ] **¹/₄ teaspoon baking powder**
- [ ] **1 tablespoon caster sugar**
- [ ] **125 g (4 oz) chilled butter, cubed**
- [ ] **1 egg yolk, lightly beaten**
- [ ] **2 tablespoons iced water**

FILLING
- [ ] **250 g (8 oz) mascarpone or cream cheese**
- [ ] **2 tablespoons icing sugar, sifted**
- [ ] **2 teaspoons ground cinnamon**
- [ ] **2 teaspoons ground mixed spice**
- [ ] **1 tablespoon Kirsch (cherry brandy)**
- [ ] **250 g (8 oz) blueberries**
- [ ] **250 g (8 oz) redcurrants**

1 Combine flour, baking powder and sugar in a mixing bowl. Rub in butter, using fingertips, until mixture resembles coarse breadcrumbs. Stir in egg yolk and enough water to mix to a firm dough, using a round-bladed knife. Knead dough on a lightly floured surface until smooth. Wrap in plastic food wrap and refrigerate for 1 hour.
2 Roll out pastry and line 12 individual loose-based 10 cm (4 in) flan tins. Prick bases and sides with a fork, line with baking paper and dried beans, and blind bake for 5 minutes. Remove baking beans and paper and bake for 5-8 minutes longer or until golden. Set aside to cool.
3 To make the filling, place mascarpone, icing sugar, cinnamon, mixed spice and Kirsch in a mixing bowl and beat until smooth. Cover and refrigerate until required. Just prior to serving, spoon mascarpone mixture into cooled pastry cases and top with blueberries and redcurrants.

FAST FEASTS

When time is short and aspirations high, try one of these fast and fabulous meals. They all taste wonderful and some look and taste as if they have taken hours to prepare. Perfect for unexpected guests, or for an easy indulgence.

BANANA MOUSSE

Light, fluffy and creamy, this mousse takes next to no time to make and is the perfect finish to any meal.

Serves 8

- [ ] **3 eggs, separated**
- [ ] **100 g (3¹/₂ oz) caster sugar**
- [ ] **4 tablespoons coconut cream**
- [ ] **3 small ripe bananas, peeled and chopped**
- [ ] **1 tablespoon lemon juice**
- [ ] **1 teaspoon ground cinnamon**
- [ ] **1 tablespoon Marsala**
- [ ] **3 teaspoons gelatine dissolved in 3 tablespoons hot water and cooled**
- [ ] **250 mL (8 fl oz) double cream**

1   Place egg yolks and caster sugar in a mixing bowl and beat until thick and creamy.
2   Place coconut cream, bananas, lemon juice, cinnamon and Marsala in a food processor or blender and process until smooth. Blend cooled gelatine mixture into egg yolk mixture, then stir in coconut mixture.
3   Place cream in a bowl and beat until soft peaks form, then fold in banana mixture. Beat egg whites until stiff peaks form and fold in banana mixture. Spoon into eight individual serving glasses and refrigerate until firm.

SMOKED SALMON BREADSTICK

A happy marriage of all the best ingredients, this filled baguette is a meal in itself.

Serves 4

- [ ] **1 long French baguette**
- [ ] **2 teaspoons Dijon mustard**
- [ ] **1 teaspoon lemon juice**
- [ ] **3 hard-boiled eggs, peeled and sliced**
- [ ] **2 tablespoons capers, drained and chopped**
- [ ] **315 g (10 oz) smoked salmon slices**
- [ ] **1 red onion, thinly sliced**
- [ ] **45 g (1¹/₂ oz) snow pea sprouts or watercress**
- [ ] **freshly ground black pepper**

1   Slice baguette in half horizontally and remove some of the centre. Combine mustard and lemon juice and spread over inside of bread.
2   Place eggs on mustard mixture on bottom half of baguette, top with capers, salmon, onion and snow pea sprouts or watercress. Season to taste with black pepper and cover with bread top. Tie at intervals with string and cut into four to serve.

Smoked Salmon Breadstick, Banana Mousse

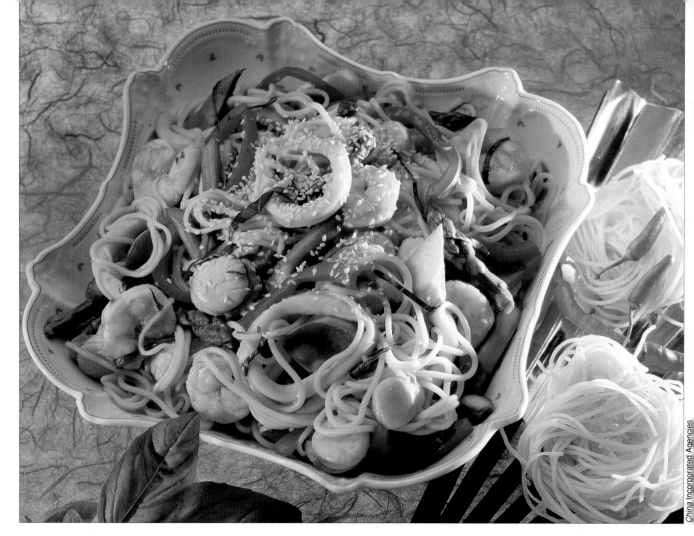

Stir-Fry Noodles with Seafood

❦

STIR-FRY NOODLES WITH SEAFOOD

The flavours and ingredients of the Orient combine to make this fast feast. Vary the vegetables according to what is available and how indulgent you feel.

Serves 4

- [ ] **375 g (12 oz) fresh egg noodles**
- [ ] **2 tablespoons sesame oil**
- [ ] **1 clove garlic, crushed**
- [ ] **2 small red chillies, finely chopped**
- [ ] **1 teaspoon grated fresh ginger**
- [ ] **500 g (1 lb) large uncooked prawns, peeled and deveined**
- [ ] **250 g (8 oz) scallops**
- [ ] **250 g (8 oz) squid hoods, sliced**
- [ ] **1/2 red pepper, cut into thin strips**
- [ ] **60 g (2 oz) mangetout, cut diagonally into 2.5 cm (1 in) pieces**
- [ ] **250 g (8 oz) asparagus spears, cut into 2.5 cm (1 in) pieces**
- [ ] **1 tablespoon finely shredded fresh basil**
- [ ] **2 tablespoons sesame seeds, toasted**

SAUCE
- [ ] **1 tablespoon cornflour**
- [ ] **1 tablespoon sugar**
- [ ] **3 tablespoons tomato sauce**
- [ ] **1 teaspoon oyster sauce**
- [ ] **1 tablespoon Worcestershire sauce**
- [ ] **250 mL (8 fl oz) water**

1 Place noodles in a large saucepan of boiling water and cook for 3 minutes or until tender. Drain, then rinse under hot water. Spread out on absorbent kitchen paper.

2 Heat oil in a frying pan or wok and cook garlic, chillies and ginger for 1 minute. Stir in prawns, scallops, squid, red pepper, mangetout, asparagus and basil and cook for 2-3 minutes, or until prawns just turn pink. Add noodles to pan and stir-fry for 1-2 minutes, or until heated through.

3 To make sauce, combine cornflour, sugar, tomato sauce, oyster sauce, Worcestershire sauce and water. Pour into pan and cook over a medium heat until sauce boils and thickens. Sprinkle with sesame seeds and serve immediately.

TIPS FOR FAST FEASTING

❦ A well-stocked pantry means that you can 'dress up' otherwise everyday foods quickly and easily.

❦ A good range of dried herbs and spices and some fresh herbs grown in your garden or in a window box can quickly transform a basic dish into a taste sensation.

❦ Look out for new Asian and Middle Eastern spice combinations.

❦ Keep a variety of interesting oils and vinegars for marinades and dressings that will add punch to basic steak, chops or chicken.

❦ Most dressings and marinades keep well and can be made in advance.

❦ Do not be afraid to use convenience foods for a fast and fabulous meal. There is an excellent range of sauces, soups, stocks and condiments available that can enhance the simplest of foods.

CHICKEN AND CHEESE SANDWICHES

Italian focaccia bread makes a great alternative to ordinary bread. Serve these sandwiches with a green salad for a complete meal.

Serves 4

- ☐ **4 pieces focaccia bread or large pitta breads, split horizontally**
- ☐ **2 boneless chicken breast fillets**
- ☐ **15 g (¹/₂ oz) butter**
- ☐ **1 tablespoon olive oil**
- ☐ **1 clove garlic, unpeeled**
- ☐ **4 slices ham**
- ☐ **8 slices Swiss cheese, such as Gruyère or Emmenthal**
- ☐ **1 tablespoon snipped fresh chives**
- ☐ **1 tablespoon finely chopped fresh dill**
- ☐ **freshly ground black pepper**

1 Trim chicken fillets. Slice each fillet horizontally to give 4 slices. Pound each slice to flatten.

2 Heat butter, oil and unpeeled clove garlic in a large heavy-based frying pan. Cook chicken, 2 slices at a time, for 1-2 minutes each side.

3 Place a slice of chicken on the bottom half of each focaccia or pitta bread. Top with a slice of ham and a slice of cheese. Place a slice of cheese on top half of each piece of focaccia.

4 Place focaccia or pitta bread halves under a hot grill and cook until cheese melts. Sprinkle chives and dill on bottom halves. Season to taste with black pepper. Place top halves of foccacia or pitta bread on bottom halves and serve immediately.

RED PEPPERED BEEF

A quick and easy Chinese dish with a medley of flavours and textures, which is sure to be popular. Serve with boiled or steamed rice and a side dish of fresh steamed vegetables.

Serves 4

- ☐ **500 g (1 lb) rump steak, cut into thin strips**
- ☐ **2 teaspoons cornflour**
- ☐ **2 tablespoons soy sauce**
- ☐ **2 tablespoons groundnut or vegetable oil**
- ☐ **2 red peppers, cut into thin strips**
- ☐ **1 small red chilli, finely chopped**
- ☐ **1 clove garlic, crushed**
- ☐ **4 spring onions, cut into 5 cm (2 in) lengths**
- ☐ **2 teaspoons grated fresh ginger**
- ☐ **1 teaspoon sugar**
- ☐ **2 tablespoons dry sherry**

1 Sprinkle meat strips with cornflour and 2 tablespoons soy sauce. Toss to coat and set aside to stand for 5 minutes.

2 Heat 1 tablespoon oil in a frying pan or wok, add red peppers, chilli, garlic, spring onions and ginger and cook for 2-3 minutes. Remove from pan and set aside.

3 Heat remaining oil in wok or frying pan and stir-fry meat for 2-3 minutes. Return pepper mixture to pan. Combine remaining soy sauce, sugar and sherry and pour into pan. Stir-fry for 1 minute longer, then serve immediately.

Chicken and Cheese Sandwiches, Red Peppered Beef

China Noritake

SPINACH RAVIOLI WITH MASCARPONE SAUCE

This sauce also goes well with other pasta.

Serves 2

- ☐ **500 g (1 lb) fresh spinach ravioli**

MASCARPONE SAUCE
- ☐ **2 teaspoons vegetable oil**
- ☐ **90 g (3 oz) streaky bacon, finely chopped**
- ☐ **185 mL (6 fl oz) chicken stock**
- ☐ **185 g (6 oz) mascarpone or cream cheese**
- ☐ **8 sun-dried tomatoes, chopped**
- ☐ **1 tablespoon finely chopped fresh basil**
- ☐ **1 tablespoon snipped fresh chives**
- ☐ **freshly ground black pepper**
- ☐ **grated fresh Parmesan cheese**

1   Cook ravioli in boiling water in a large saucepan for 4-5 minutes, or tender. Drain and set aside to keep warm.
2   To make sauce, heat oil in a small saucepan and cook bacon for 2-3 minutes. Stir in stock, mascarpone or cream cheese and sun-dried tomatoes, and simmer for 5 minutes, or until sauce reduces and thickens. Stir in basil, chives, and black pepper to taste. Spoon sauce over pasta, toss to coat, sprinkle with Parmesan cheese and serve immediately.

LIQUEUR STRAWBERRY PUDDING

This quick and easy dessert looks and tastes as if it has taken hours to prepare.

Serves 4

- ☐ **250 g (8 oz) strawberries, hulled and sliced lengthways**
- ☐ **4 tablespoons Grand Marnier (orange liqueur)**
- ☐ **3 eggs, separated**
- ☐ **250 g (8 oz) mascarpone or cream cheese**
- ☐ **1 tablespoon caster sugar**
- ☐ **100 g (3½ oz) amaretti biscuits, crushed**

1   Place strawberries and liqueur in a bowl and set aside to marinate for 30 minutes.
2   Place egg yolks and mascarpone or cream cheese in a bowl and beat until smooth. Beat egg whites until soft peaks form, then gradually beat in sugar. Fold egg white mixture into cheese mixture.
3   Divide half the cheese mixture between four individual serving dishes, sprinkle half the biscuits over mixture then top with strawberries and remaining cheese mixture. Finally sprinkle with remaining biscuits. Cover with plastic food wrap and refrigerate until required.

COMBINATION NOODLE SOUP

A Chinese-style main meal soup that uses canned consommé as its base, is a quick and tasty dish when time is short.

Serves 6

- ☐ **2 teaspoons groundnut or vegetable oil**
- ☐ **1 onion, finely chopped**
- ☐ **1 red pepper, finely chopped**
- ☐ **2 x 440 g (14 oz) canned chicken consommé**
- ☐ **500 mL (16 fl oz) water**
- ☐ **2 chicken breast fillets, cooked and thinly sliced**
- ☐ **375 g (12 oz) Chinese barbecued pork fillet, thinly sliced**
- ☐ **12 small uncooked prawns, peeled and deveined**
- ☐ **100 g (3½ oz) rice noodles, cooked**
- ☐ **75 g (2½ oz) oyster mushrooms, sliced**
- ☐ **75 g (2½ oz) canned bamboo shoots, drained and sliced**
- ☐ **4 lettuce leaves, shredded**
- ☐ **1 tablespoon finely chopped fresh coriander**
- ☐ **freshly ground black pepper**

1   Heat oil in a large saucepan and cook onion and red pepper for 5 minutes or until soft.
2   Add chicken consomme and water and bring to the boil. Reduce heat and add chicken, pork, prawns, rice noodles, mushrooms and bamboo shoots. Simmer for 5 minutes, or until prawns turn pink and are cooked. Stir in lettuce, coriander, and black pepper to taste. Serve immediately.

Spinach Ravioli with Mascarpone Sauce, Liqueur Strawberry Pudding, Combination Noodle Soup

45

QUICK AND CASUAL

This section is full of recipes suitable for quick, casual meals. Many can be cooked on the barbecue or under the grill and are suitable for both experienced and inexperienced cooks.

CHILLI SEAFOOD SKEWERS

When cooking on a barbecue, oil the grill so that the food does not stick to it.

Serves 4

- ☐ **8 large uncooked prawns, peeled and deveined with tails left intact**
- ☐ **8 scallops**
- ☐ **500 g (1 lb) white fish fillet, such as cod or monkfish, skinned and cut into 8 x 2.5 cm (1 in) cubes**
- ☐ **500 g (1 lb) salmon fillet, skinned and cut into 8 x 2.5 cm (1 in) cubes**
- ☐ **8 mussels, removed from shells**
- ☐ **8 bamboo skewers**

MARINADE
- ☐ **4 tablespoons vegetable oil**
- ☐ **3 red chillies, finely chopped**
- ☐ **2 cloves garlic, crushed**
- ☐ **2 tablespoons lemon juice**

1   Oil eight wooden skewers. Push point of a skewer through tail end of a prawn. Thread on a scallop and then push skewer through top of prawn. Thread a piece of white fish, a mussel and a piece of salmon onto skewer. Repeat with remaining seafood and skewers.

2   To make marinade, combine oil, chillies, garlic and lemon juice in a bowl. Place skewers on a hot barbecue or under a hot grill and brush with marinade. Cook, turning frequently, until seafood changes colour and is cooked through. Serve immediately.

China Bohemia Crystal

Chilli Seafood Skewers, Thai Lime Poussin (page 48)

THAI LIME POUSSIN

Evoke the taste of Thailand, with tender poussin marinated in lime juice, coriander and coconut milk.

Serves 4

- ☐ **4 poussin**

MARINADE
- ☐ **3 tablespoons lime juice**
- ☐ **2 tablespoons chopped fresh coriander**
- ☐ **250 mL (8 fl oz) coconut milk**
- ☐ **1 red chilli, chopped**
- ☐ **2 tablespoons honey**
- ☐ **freshly ground black pepper**

1 Cut poussin down middle of backs and flatten. Thread a skewer through wings and a skewer through legs of each.
2 To make marinade, place lime juice, coriander, coconut milk, chilli, honey, and black pepper to taste in a large baking dish. Mix to combine. Place poussin flesh side down in marinade. Cover and refrigerate for 4 hours or overnight.
3 Cook on a hot barbecue or under a hot grill, basting frequently with marinade. Cook 15 minutes each side, or until tender and cooked through.

RAINBOW TROUT WITH DILL BUTTER

Trout is delicious and versatile. Served with a herb butter, it makes a fast and impressive main dish cooked on the barbecue or in the oven.

Serves 4
Oven temperature 180°C, 350°F, Gas 4

- ☐ **4 rainbow trout, cleaned**

DILL BUTTER
- ☐ **90 g (3 oz) butter, softened**
- ☐ **2 tablespoons chopped fresh dill**
- ☐ **1 clove garlic, crushed**
- ☐ **2 teaspoons grated lemon rind**

1 To make Dill Butter, place butter, dill, garlic and lemon rind in a bowl and mix until combined.
2 Place trout on individual pieces of foil large enough to enclose trout. Spread each trout with Dill Butter and wrap foil around trout to enclose. Place parcels on barbecue and cook for 10 minutes each side, or bake in oven for 15 minutes, or until fish flakes when tested.

Right: Italian Beef Rolls, Spicy Mint Lamb Riblets
Below: Rainbow Trout with Dill Butter

China Villeroy & Boch

ITALIAN BEEF ROLLS

*Tender slices of steak wrapped around
a cheese and tomato filling.*

Serves 4

- [ ] **4 thin rump or sirloin steaks**
- [ ] **8 spinach leaves, stalks removed**
- [ ] **16 cherry tomatoes**

CHEESE FILLING
- [ ] **60 g (2 oz) grated mozzarella
cheese**
- [ ] **125 g (4 oz) ricotta cheese**
- [ ] **1 tablespoon chopped fresh
parsley**
- [ ] **freshly ground black pepper**

1   Trim all visible fat from meat. Place
meat on a board, cover with plastic food
wrap and pound, using a mallet, until thin.
Divide spinach into four portions and
spread in a layer over each piece of steak.
2   To make filling, combine mozzarella,
ricotta, parsley, and black pepper to taste.
Spread over spinach, then place cherry
tomatoes across middle of filling and roll
up. Secure with toothpicks. Barbecue,
turning on a hot, oiled plate for 10 minutes,
or until cooked through.

SPICY MINT LAMB RIBLETS

*This recipe uses tender young lamb
riblets rather than pork or beef ribs,
making a quickly prepared dish. Serve
with a green salad and crusty bread for
a complete meal.*

Serves 4
Oven temperature 180°C, 350°F, Gas 4

- [ ] **2 lamb breasts, cut into riblets**

MARINADE
- [ ] **170 g (5¹/₂ oz) mint jelly**
- [ ] **2 tablespoons Worcestershire
sauce**
- [ ] **1 teaspoon chilli powder**
- [ ] **2 teaspoons finely chopped fresh
rosemary**
- [ ] **freshly ground black pepper**

1   To make marinade, place mint jelly,
Worcestershire sauce, chilli powder,
rosemary, and black pepper to taste in a
bowl and mix to combine. Place riblets in
a large baking dish and pour marinade
over. Cover and refrigerate overnight.
2   Remove cover and bake riblets for 20
minutes, or until cooked through and
tender. Transfer ribs to a hot barbecue or
grill and cook for 5-10 minutes longer, or
until browned. Brush frequently with
marinade during cooking.

DROP SCONES

Stacks of warm scones with maple syrup and accompanied by thick cream.

Makes 10

- ☐ **125 g (4 oz) self-raising flour, sifted**
- ☐ **2 tablespoons sugar**
- ☐ **1 egg, lightly beaten**
- ☐ **185 mL (6 fl oz) milk**
- ☐ **maple syrup**

1 Place flour and sugar in a bowl. Mix in egg and milk until smooth. Cook tablespoons of mixture in a heated greased heavy-based frying pan. Turn when bubbles appear on the surface.

2 Place scones in a stack and top with maple syrup.

NUT FLAN

The combination of nuts and spices tastes wonderful in this easy-to-make baked flan. Eaten hot, warm or cold, it is absolutely delicious and would make the perfect dessert for a barbecue.

Serves 12
Oven temperature 220°C, 425°F, Gas 7

SPICED PASTRY
- ☐ **185 g (6 oz) plain flour, sifted**
- ☐ **¼ teaspoon baking powder**
- ☐ **1 teaspoon ground mixed spice**
- ☐ **1 tablespoon caster sugar**
- ☐ **125 g (4 oz) chilled butter, cubed**
- ☐ **1 egg yolk, lightly beaten**
- ☐ **1 tablespoon iced water**

NUT FILLING
- ☐ **60 g (2 oz) butter**
- ☐ **90 g (3 oz) brown sugar**
- ☐ **1 teaspoon vanilla essence**
- ☐ **3 eggs**
- ☐ **185 mL (6 fl oz) golden syrup**
- ☐ **2 tablespoons plain flour, sifted**
- ☐ **1 teaspoon ground mixed spice**
- ☐ **1 teaspoon ground cinnamon**
- ☐ **200 g (6½ oz) roasted macadamia or pecan nuts, roughly chopped**

1 To make pastry, combine flour, baking powder, mixed spice and sugar in a mixing bowl. Rub in butter with fingertips until mixture resembles coarse breadcrumbs. Stir in egg yolk and enough water to mix to a firm dough, using a round-bladed knife. Knead dough lightly on a floured surface until smooth. Wrap in plastic food wrap and refrigerate for 1 hour.

China Limoges

2   Roll out pastry and line a greased 25 cm (10 in) flan tin. Prick base and sides with a fork and line with baking paper and uncooked beans. Bake blind for 5 minutes, then remove beans and paper and cook pastry for 8 minutes longer. Set aside to cool.

3   To make filling, beat butter, sugar and vanilla essence until light and fluffy. Add eggs one at a time beating well after each addition. Fold in golden syrup, flour, mixed spice, cinnamon and macadamia or pecan nuts. Spoon filling into flan case and bake at 160°C (325°F, Gas 3) for 35-40 minutes or until firm.

Drop Scones, Macadamia Flan

China Incorporated Agencies

Smoked Salmon Brioches

🍂

SMOKED SALMON BRIOCHES

If brioches are unavailable, you might like to use small bread rolls for this recipe.

Serves 6

☐   **6 small brioches**

SALMON FILLING
☐   **200 g (6¹/₂ oz) cream cheese**
☐   **4 tablespoons sour cream**
☐   **1 tablespoon capers, chopped**
☐   **2 teaspoons chopped fresh dill**
☐   **6 slices smoked salmon, chopped**
☐   **2 teaspoons lemon juice**

1   Cut top from brioches, scoop out centre and discard. Set brioches aside.

2   To make filling, place cream cheese and sour cream in a bowl and beat until light and smooth. Fold in capers, dill, salmon and lemon juice. Spoon filling into brioches and replace with tops.

TABLE SETTING

Simple household items, such as bed sheets and ribbons, can inexpensively transform any table into a lavish setting. All it takes is a little know-how.

AN INDULGENT TABLE

Our round table for four has a diameter of 122 cm (4 ft).

MATERIALS
- [ ] **1 white sheet, 1.4 x 2.2 m (4¹/₂ x 7 ft)**
- [ ] **1 patterned sheet, 1.4 x 2.2 m (4¹/₂ x 7 ft)**
- [ ] **double-sided tape**
- [ ] **4 lengths of 5 cm (2 in) wide ribbon, each 1.40 m (56 in)**
- [ ] **4 small gifts**
- [ ] **pink wrapping paper**
- [ ] **3 m (11¹/₂ ft) of 1 cm (¹/₂ in) wide ribbon**
- [ ] **4 napkins (paper or linen)**

METHOD

1   Press both sheets well to remove any creases. Cover table with white sheet. To make the sheet hang evenly on the round table, fold each corner under to the wrong side and tape it up with double-sided tape.

2   Cover white sheet with patterned sheet. Fold point of each corner inside to allow white sheet to extend below. Tape up with double-sided tape. Gather each corner of pattern sheet and tie with one length of 1.40 m (56 in) ribbon. Tie ribbon into a bow. Neaten ends of bow by cutting a 'fish-tail'.

3   Wrap individual gifts in pink wrapping paper and tie with 1 cm (¹/₂ in) wide ribbon. Place at each place setting.

4   Fold napkins and position at each place.

FINAL DETAILS

The napkins have been folded to form what is known as a Bishop's Hat.

1   Fold napkin into a triangle. Centre of triangle points down.

2   Fold right-hand and left-hand corners down to centre point.

3   Fold top corner down 10 cm (4 in), towards bottom point.

4   Fold folded point back to upper edge.

5   Turn napkin over. Fold bottom edges to overlap and tuck inside at back.

6   Stand napkin and turn down two outer points.

The centrepiece for this table is a silver teapot – a family treasure – filled with tiny bud roses. A handmade doily complements the arrangement.

A small gift of soap for each person is a pleasure to receive as well as delicately scenting the room. Other gift ideas are small pouches of potpourri tied with a pretty ribbon, or an individual flower picked fresh from your garden.

NOSTALGIA FOOD

These are the meals that we all dream about. They are hearty and delicious, evoking memories of childhood days – the meals that your family and friends will love you for.

PEACH BREAD AND BUTTER TOFFEE PUDDING

Toffee poured into the base of the baking dish adds a delicious flavour to this traditional English pudding. Baking it in a pan of hot water ensures a smooth, creamy custard.

Serves 8
Oven temperature 180°C, 350°F, Gas 4

- ☐ **6 peaches, peeled, stoned and sliced**
- ☐ **45 g (1¹/₂ oz) butter, softened**
- ☐ **12 slices white bread, crusts removed**
- ☐ **3 teaspoons cinnamon**

TOFFEE
- ☐ **185 g (6 oz) sugar**
- ☐ **185 mL (6 fl oz) water**

BENEDICTINE CUSTARD
- ☐ **3 eggs**
- ☐ **155 g (5 oz) caster sugar**
- ☐ **250 mL (8 fl oz) milk, scalded**
- ☐ **250 mL (8 fl oz) double cream, scalded**
- ☐ **2 tablespoons Benedictine liqueur**

1 To make toffee, place sugar and water in a small saucepan and cook, stirring over a low heat until sugar dissolves. Increase heat and simmer until syrupy and golden. Pour toffee into base of a well greased 25 cm (10 in) round ovenproof dish.
2 Poach or microwave peaches until just tender, drain well and set aside.
3 To make custard, place eggs and sugar in a bowl and whisk to combine. Whisk in milk, cream and Benedictine and mix to combine, then strain. Butter bread on one side, then cut into triangles.
4 Place a layer of bread in base of ovenproof dish then top with a layer of peaches and sprinkle with cinnamon. Repeat layers, until bread, peaches and cinnamon are all used, ending with a bread layer. Pour custard evenly over the layers. Bake for 50-60 minutes, or until custard is set. Stand for 15 minutes before turning out and serving.

China Wedgewood *Silverware* R.P. Symons

COCONUT AND ALMOND LAMB CURRY

Flavoured with fragrant spices, this curry has a rich creamy texture. To make it really special, decorate with gold leaf, available from Asian foodstores.

Serves 6

- ☐ **3 cloves garlic, peeled**
- ☐ **1 teaspoon grated fresh ginger**
- ☐ **60 g (2 oz) blanched almonds**
- ☐ **2 tablespoons desiccated coconut, toasted**
- ☐ **3 fresh red chillies, chopped**
- ☐ **2 tablespoons ghee or oil**
- ☐ **1 large onion, finely chopped**
- ☐ **1 teaspoon ground cumin**
- ☐ **1 teaspoon ground cardamom**
- ☐ **$1/_2$ teaspoon ground fennel**
- ☐ **4 whole cloves or $1/_4$ teaspoon ground cloves**
- ☐ **1 teaspoon black mustard seeds**
- ☐ **2 tablespoons freshly chopped coriander or mint**
- ☐ **2 tomatoes, peeled and chopped**
- ☐ **$1^1/_2$ kg (3 lb) boneless leg or shoulder lamb, cubed**
- ☐ **250 mL (8 fl oz) beef stock**
- ☐ **125 mL (4 fl oz) coconut cream**
- ☐ **1 teaspoon garam masala**
- ☐ **1 tablespoon slivered almonds, toasted**
- ☐ **1 small envelope edible gold leaf (optional)**

1 Place garlic, ginger, almonds, coconut and chillies in a food processor or blender with a little water and process to form a smooth paste.

2 Heat ghee or oil in a large heavy-based frying pan and cook onion and almond paste over a low heat for 2-3 minutes, stirring occasionally. Add cumin, cardamom, fennel, cloves, mustard seeds, and coriander or mint. Cook, stirring, for 4-5 minutes longer. Stir in tomatoes, mashing well to form a pulpy mixture. Add lamb and cook over a medium-high heat, stirring well to coat meat with spice mixture. Stir in stock and bring to the boil.

3 Reduce heat, cover saucepan and simmer for 1-1$1/_2$ hours, or until lamb is tender and liquid reduces and thickens. Stir occasionally to prevent curry from sticking to pan.

4 Pour in coconut cream, sprinkle with garam marsala and cook, stirring, for 5 minutes longer. Just prior to serving sprinkle with slivered almonds, and flakes of gold leaf, if using.

SERVING SUGGESTION

Serve this tasty lamb curry with boiled basmati rice and a selection of accompaniments, such as chopped tomato and onion with mint or basil; chopped cucumber with yogurt and chopped dill; sliced banana or pineapple sprinkled with coconut; chilli pickles; or a hot mango chutney.

Accompany with poppadums, naan bread or chapatis.

Above: Steak with Seeded Mustard Sauce, Gourmet Barbecue Sausages
Right: Stilton Soup, Coconut and Almond Lamb Curry

STILTON SOUP

A creamy soup that takes only about half an hour to prepare.

Serves 6

- [ ] **30 g (1 oz) butter**
- [ ] **1 onion, finely chopped**
- [ ] **3 leeks, washed, trimmed and cut into 1 cm (¹/₂ in) thick slices**
- [ ] **750 mL (1¹/₄ pt) chicken stock**
- [ ] **1 bouquet garni**
- [ ] **1¹/₂ tablespoons cornflour blended with 3 tablespoons milk**
- [ ] **375 mL (12 fl oz) milk**
- [ ] **freshly ground black pepper**
- [ ] **200 g (6¹/₂ oz) Stilton cheese, trimmed of crust, crumbled**
- [ ] **1 tablespoon finely chopped fresh parsley**

1   Melt butter in a large saucepan and cook onion over a medium heat, for 5 minutes or until soft. Add leeks and cook for 5 minutes longer.
2   Stir in stock and bouquet garni. Bring to the boil, then reduce heat and simmer uncovered for 20 minutes.
3   Stir cornflour mixture and milk into soup and bring slowly to a simmer, stirring constantly. Stir cheese into soup then remove from heat and stir until cheese is completely melted and soup is creamy. Season to taste with black pepper. Ladle into soup bowls, sprinkle with parsley and serve immediately.

STEAK WITH SEEDED MUSTARD SAUCE

Serves 2

- [ ] **2 sirloin or fillet steaks, 2.5-5 cm (1-2 in) thick**

MUSTARD SAUCE
- [ ] **1 tablespoon wholegrain mustard**
- [ ] **250 mL (8 fl oz) cream**
- [ ] **freshly ground black pepper**
- [ ] **lemon juice to taste**

1   Fry or grill steaks until cooked to your liking. If frying steaks, remove meat from pan and keep warm. Drain meat juices from pan, leaving about 1 tablespoon in pan. If grilling steaks, melt a little butter in a small frying pan.
2   To make sauce, stir mustard into pan and cook for 1 minute. Pour in cream and cook over high heat, stirring well until sauce reduces and becomes thick and glossy. Season to taste with black pepper and lemon juice. Spoon over steaks and serve immediately.

GOURMET BARBECUE SAUSAGES

Choose from the specialty sausages available at delicatessens and butchers' shops to add an individual touch.

Serves 4
- [ ] **8 thick sausages**
- [ ] **125 mL (4 fl oz) oyster sauce**
- [ ] **2 tablespoons wholegrain mustard**
- [ ] **24 bottled oysters, drained**

1   Place sausages in a large saucepan of cold water and bring slowly to the boil. Drain and allow sausages to cool.
2   Brush sausages with oyster sauce and grill or barbecue, brushing frequently with oyster sauce, until browned and heated through. Cut each sausage halfway through, along one side. Spread a little mustard in each sausage and fill with oysters. Brush with oyster sauce and return to barbecue or grill to heat through.

❦
STANDING RIB ROAST WITH HORSERADISH

In this Master Class you learn how to cook the perfect roast meal and how to make individual Yorkshire Puddings to add that finishing touch.

Serves 6
Oven temperature 190°C, 375°F, Gas 5

- [ ] **2 kg (4 lb) prime rib of beef on the bone**
- [ ] **45 g (1½ oz) butter, softened**
- [ ] **4 tablespoons vegetable oil**
- [ ] **freshly ground black pepper**
- [ ] **6 potatoes, peeled and halved**
- [ ] **3 carrots, peeled and halved**
- [ ] **6 onions, peeled**
- [ ] **3 parsnips, peeled and halved**
- [ ] **170 mL (5½ oz) beef stock**

YORKSHIRE PUDDINGS
- [ ] **90 g (3 oz) plain flour, sifted**
- [ ] **freshly ground black pepper**
- [ ] **1 egg, lightly beaten**
- [ ] **4 tablespoons milk**
- [ ] **3 tablespoons water**
- [ ] **1½ tablespoons beef dripping**

HORSERADISH SAUCE
- [ ] **125 mL (4 fl oz) double cream**
- [ ] **1 tablespoon horseradish relish**
- [ ] **freshly ground black pepper**

1   Place beef in a baking tin, fat side up. Spread with butter and pour over 2 tablespoons oil. Bake for 30 minutes, basting with juices every 10 minutes. Heat remaining oil in another baking tin on top of cooker and cook potatoes until brown on all sides.

2   When beef has cooked for 30 minutes, place baking dish with potatoes on top shelf of oven and place carrots, onions and parsnips around beef. Cook for 15 minutes then turn vegetables over. Baste beef and vegetables with pan juices and cook for 15 minutes longer. Season to taste with black pepper and pour in stock. Increase oven temperature to 220°C, (425°F, Gas 7) and cook for 15 minutes longer for rare beef, or 30 minutes longer for medium-rare beef. Transfer to a serving platter and allow to rest in a warm place for 10 minutes before carving. Reserve baking tin and juices.

3   To make Yorkshire Puddings, sift flour into a bowl. Add black pepper to taste and make a well in the centre. Combine egg, milk and water and pour into flour mixture.

Beat slowly to incorporate wet ingredients into dry ingredients. Place 1 teaspoon beef dripping in six deep tartlet tins and heat in oven until dripping is sizzling. Divide pudding batter between tartlet tins and cook at 220°C (425°F, Gas 7) for 20-25 minutes, or until puffed and golden.

4   Skim fat off pan juices from baking tin. Heat gently on top of cooker, stirring to scrape up caramelised juices. Add extra stock or water if required and cook until reduced to a sauce consistency. Pour into a sauce boat and set aside to keep warm.

5   To make Horseradish Sauce, whip cream until soft peaks form. Fold in horseradish relish and season to taste with black pepper.

Place beef dripping in patty pans and heat in oven until dripping is sizzling.

Divide pudding batter between patty pans and cook until puffed and golden.

China Royal Doulton

OUTDOOR PLEASURES

Use any excuse that occurs to you, pack all you need – good food, plates, mugs and cutlery, cushions and folding chairs – and take off for a wonderful picnic or barbecue away from home.

LOBSTER TAILS WITH PISTACHIO BUTTER

There is something wonderfully extravagant and primitive about grilling lobster outdoors. If your outdoor party is by the sea, all the better.

Serves 6

- ☐ **6 uncooked lobster tails**

PISTACHIO BUTTER
- ☐ **185 g (6 oz) butter, softened**
- ☐ **3 tablespoons chopped, shelled, unsalted pistachio nuts**
- ☐ **2 tablespoons finely chopped fresh parsley**
- ☐ **1 tablespoon finely snipped fresh chives**
- ☐ **1 teaspoon lemon juice**
- ☐ **1 tablespoon finely chopped fresh sage**
- ☐ **freshly ground black pepper**

1   To make Pistachio Butter, place butter in a small bowl and beat until soft and smooth. Add pistachios, parsley, chives, sage, lemon juice, and black pepper to taste and mix to combine.
2   Spread each lobster tail with a little butter mixture and place on a hot barbecue or under a hot grill. Cook for 5-10 minutes, or until cooked through, turning once and basting frequently with butter during cooking. Serve topped with remaining butter.

POTATO AND DILL SALAD

A luscious rich potato salad that goes well with barbecued lobster or any grilled meats.

Serves 6-8

- ☐ **1 kg (2 lb) new potatoes**
- ☐ **3 spring onions, sliced**
- ☐ **2 tablespoons finely chopped fresh dill**
- ☐ **250 mL (8 fl oz) sour cream**

VINAIGRETTE
- ☐ **2 teaspoons Dijon mustard**
- ☐ **1¹/₂ tablespoons white wine vinegar**
- ☐ **125 mL (4 fl oz) olive oil**
- ☐ **freshly ground black pepper**

1   Boil or microwave potatoes until just tender. Drain and refresh under cold running water. Drain again and cut potatoes in half. Place in a bowl. Add spring onions and dill and toss to combine.
2   To make Vinaigrette, place mustard, vinegar, oil, and black pepper to taste in a food processor or blender and process until combined. Pour over warm potatoes, add sour cream and toss gently to coat potatoes. Transfer to a serving bowl and serve at room temperature.

Lobster Tails with Pistachio Butter, Potato and Dill Salad

SMOKED CHICKEN SALAD WITH GINGER DRESSING

A pretty salad with a fresh taste that is easy to make and travels well. Put the salad in the serving bowl to marinate on the way to your picnic.

Serves 6

- ☐ **1 smoked chicken, 1-1.5 kg (2-3 lb), meat removed and cut into bite-size pieces**
- ☐ **4 spring onions, finely chopped**
- ☐ **1 small red pepper, finely sliced**
- ☐ **1 small red chilli, seeded and finely sliced**
- ☐ **1 tablespoon chopped fresh coriander**
- ☐ **1 tablespoon chopped fresh mint**
- ☐ **freshly ground black pepper**

ORANGE AND GINGER DRESSING
- ☐ **3 tablespoons olive oil**
- ☐ **2 tablespoons white wine vinegar**
- ☐ **2 tablespoons freshly squeezed orange juice**
- ☐ **1 teaspoon wholegrain mustard**
- ☐ **1 teaspoon brown sugar**
- ☐ **1 teaspoon finely grated fresh ginger**

1   Place chicken, spring onions, red pepper, chilli, coriander and mint in a serving bowl. Season to taste with black pepper.

2   To make dressing, place oil, vinegar, orange juice, mustard, sugar and ginger in a screwtop jar and shake well to combine. Pour over chicken mixture and toss to combine. Cover and refrigerate.

BAKED CAMEMBERT AND GORGONZOLA LOAF

Bake this loaf within the hour before you leave for your picnic. It is wrapped in foil and will stay warm.

Serves 6
Oven temperature 180°C, 350°F, Gas 4

- ☐ **23 cm (9 in) round loaf of bread**
- ☐ **375 g (12 oz) Camembert cheese, sliced thinly**
- ☐ **200 g (6¹/₂ oz) Gorgonzola cheese, sliced thinly**
- ☐ **3 pears, peeled, cored and sliced thinly**
- ☐ **3 fresh dates, thinly sliced**

1   Slice top from bread and scoop out centre, leaving a 2.5 cm (1 in) shell. Top and centre of bread can be reserved and made into breadcrumbs for later use.

2   Place a layer of Camembert cheese slices over base of bread and top with a layer of Gorgonzola cheese and a layer of pear slices. Repeat layers, finishing with a layer of pears. Wrap loaf in a sheet of aluminium foil and bake for 30 minutes.

3   Remove from oven, open foil and top with dates. Rewrap while still hot for transportation to picnic. Serve directly from the foil.

BROWNIES

Dense rich chocolate brownies studded with walnuts and topped with rich chocolate icing are the perfect sweet finish to any barbecue or picnic.

Makes 24
Oven temperature 180°C, 350°F, Gas 4

- ☐ **125 g (4 oz) dark chocolate, roughly chopped**
- ☐ **125 g (4 oz) unsalted butter, cubed**
- ☐ **1 teaspoon vanilla essence**
- ☐ **2 eggs**
- ☐ **220 g (7 oz) caster sugar**
- ☐ **125 g (4 oz) plain flour, sifted**
- ☐ **¹/₄ teaspoon baking powder**
- ☐ **125 g (4 oz) walnuts, chopped**

CHOCOLATE FUDGE ICING
- ☐ **200 g (6¹/₂ oz) dark chocolate, melted**
- ☐ **45 g (1¹/₂ oz) butter, melted**

1   Melt chocolate and butter in a bowl over a saucepan of simmering water, taking care not to overheat. Remove from heat and stir in vanilla.

2   Beat eggs and sugar together until thick and creamy. Fold into chocolate mixture. Sift flour and baking powder over chocolate mixture. Sprinkle walnuts over chocolate mixture, then fold in using a spatula.

3   Spoon into a greased and lined 20 cm (8 in) square shallow cake tin. Smooth top using spatula. Bake for 25-30 minutes, or until only just set. Cool in pan on a wire rack.

4   To make icing, combine chocolate and butter in a mixing bowl and beat until well blended. Spread over brownie and set aside to firm. Cut into 24 squares to serve.

Smoked Chicken Salad with Ginger Dressing, Baked Camembert and Gorgonzola Loaf, Brownies

CHICKEN LIVER TERRINE WITH BLUEBERRIES

Coarsely textured, this terrine is packed with strong, distinctive flavours. Serve with crusty bread, a salad and fresh fruit for a complete outdoor meal.

Serves 6
Oven temperature 200°C, 400°F, Gas 6

- [ ] **750 g (1¹⁄₂ lb) fresh chicken or duck livers, cleaned**
- [ ] **freshly ground black pepper**
- [ ] **¹⁄₄ teaspoon nutmeg**
- [ ] **¹⁄₄ teaspoon five spice powder**
- [ ] **¹⁄₄ teaspoon sugar**
- [ ] **4 tablespoons sherry**
- [ ] **8 very thin slices prosciutto or bacon**
- [ ] **4 lean bacon rashers, chopped**
- [ ] **500 g (1 lb) minced pork**
- [ ] **185 mL (6 fl oz) white wine**
- [ ] **440 g (14 oz) canned blueberries, drained**
- [ ] **2 bay leaves**

Line a terrine with prosciutto or bacon.

1   Place livers in a bowl and cover with lukewarm water. Set aside to soak for 1 hour.

2   Drain livers and place in a clean bowl. Add black pepper to taste, nutmeg, five spice powder, sugar and sherry. Toss to combine all ingredients. Cover with plastic food wrap and refrigerate for 4 hours.

3   Line a greased 23 x 10 cm (9 x 4 in) terrine or loaf dish with prosciutto or bacon allowing slices to overhang the top. Mince one-third of marinated livers with bacon. Combine with pork and wine, and season to taste with black pepper. Spread one-third of this mixture into base of terrine. Top with half the remaining livers and scatter with half the blueberries. Cover with another one-third of the minced mixture. Top with remaining blueberries, then another layer of livers, finally finishing with remaining minced mixture. Cover with a slice of prosciutto or bacon and fold overhanging slices into the centre to cover the filling. Place bay leaves on top and cover tightly with lid or foil.

Mince one-third of livers with bacon, combine with pork and wine and season with black pepper.

4   Place in a baking dish with enough hot water to come halfway up sides of dish and cook for 1¹⁄₂-1³⁄₄ hours, or until mixture is coming away from sides of dish and is brown around edges.

5   Remove lid, drain off excess liquid and set aside to cool. To serve, turn out and cut into slices.

Fill terrine with alternate layers of mince mixture, livers and blueberries.

NAUGHTY BUT NICE

What could be more indulgent than Passion Fruit Petit Fours! Try Cheese Cigars with Coriander Pesto as a tasty pre-dinner treat. For those who really want the ultimate indulgence, see the Master Class and make the Surprise Truffle Bag.

TOFFEE TOPPED MINIATURE PARIS BREST

Choux pastry is easy to make. Just remember, do not tip the flour in before the water mixture is boiling and do not add all the eggs at once.

Makes 18
Oven temperature 220°C, 425°F, Gas 7

CHOUX PASTRY
☐ **250 mL (8 fl oz) water**
☐ **75 g (2¹/₂ oz) butter, cut into small pieces**
☐ **90 g (3 oz) plain flour, sifted**
☐ **3 eggs**

FILLING
☐ **200 mL (6¹/₂ fl oz) double cream, whipped**
☐ **250 g (8 oz) diced fresh fruits**

TOFFEE
☐ **220 g (7 oz) caster sugar**
☐ **4 tablespoons water**
☐ **icing sugar for dusting**

1   To make pastry, place water and butter in a saucepan and slowly bring to the boil. As soon as the mixture boils, quickly stir in flour, using a wooden spoon. Cook over a low heat, stirring constantly for 2 minutes, or until mixture is smooth and leaves sides of pan. Remove from heat and set aside to cool slightly. Beat in eggs, one at a time, beating well after each addition and until mixture is light and glossy.

2   Line baking trays with baking paper and trace 18 x 5 cm (2 in) circles on it, then turn paper . Spoon pastry mixture into a piping bag fitted with a 1 cm (¹/₂ in) plain nozzle. Pipe two rows of pastry, one on top of the other, inside the traced circles. Dust with icing sugar and bake for 8 minutes. Prop open oven door using the handle of a wooden spoon and cook pastries for 10 minutes longer, or until golden and crisp. Remove from tray and cool on a wire rack. Split pastries in half, using a bread knife. Return to the oven and bake at 120°C (250°F/Gas ¹/₂) for 5 minutes or until pastries dry out.

3   Fill bottom halves with whipped cream and top with fruit. Replace lids and set aside.

4   To make toffee, place sugar and water in a small saucepan. Cook over a medium heat stirring constantly until sugar dissolves. Continue to cook without stirring until mixture is golden. Remove from heat and stand until bubbles subside. Spin or spoon toffee over pastries to decorate. Serve within an hour.

Toffee Topped Miniature Paris Brest

CHEESE CIGARS WITH CORIANDER PESTO

A pesto made of coriander is the perfect accompaniment to these tasty Cheese Cigars – serve as an indulgent snack or as a pre-dinner treat.

Makes 12

- ☐ **12 slices white bread, crusts removed**
- ☐ **2 teaspoons prepared English mustard**
- ☐ **4 tablespoons finely grated fresh Parmesan cheese**
- ☐ **60 g (2 oz) grated mozzarella cheese**
- ☐ **1 tablespoon snipped fresh chives**
- ☐ **cayenne pepper**
- ☐ **1 egg, lightly beaten**
- ☐ **vegetable oil for cooking**

CORIANDER PESTO
- ☐ **3 large bunches fresh coriander**
- ☐ **2 cloves garlic, crushed**
- ☐ **60 g (2 oz) pine nuts**
- ☐ **125 mL (4 fl oz) olive oil**
- ☐ **60 g (2 oz) grated fresh Parmesan cheese**

1   Roll each slice of bread with a rolling pin, to flatten as much as possible.
2   Combine mustard, Parmesan cheese, mozzarella cheese, chives, and cayenne pepper to taste in a bowl. Divide mixture between bread slices and spread over half of each bread slice. Brush unspread sides of bread slices with egg. Roll each slice up tightly using the egg to seal rolls. Arrange side by side on a tray. Cover and refrigerate until ready to cook.
3   Heat 2 cm (1 in) of oil in a frying pan. When hot, cook cigars a few at a time until evenly golden all over. Drain on absorbent kitchen paper.
4   To make pesto, place coriander leaves, garlic and pine nuts in a food processor or blender and process until finely chopped. With machine running slowly, pour in oil and process mixture until smooth. Add cheese and process to blend. Serve with hot cigars.

CHOCOLATE PASTILLES WITH FRUITS AND NUTS

Makes 32

- ☐ **250 g (8 oz) dark chocolate, melted and cooled slightly**
- ☐ **90 g (3 oz) dried pineapple, chopped**
- ☐ **45 g (1½ oz) dried banana chips, roughly crushed**
- ☐ **16 glacé cherries, chopped**
- ☐ **3 tablespoons flaked almonds**

1   Line two baking trays with baking paper. Drop 32 spoonfuls of melted chocolate onto trays leaving 10 cm (4 in) between each. Quickly spread each spoonful into a flat disc using the back of a spoon. Stick pineapple, banana chips, cherries and almonds upright in chocolate and refrigerate until set.
2   Carefully remove pastilles from paper using a spatula. Store in airtight containers.

DOUBLE-INDULGENT FUDGE

Layered fudge studded with nuts – each piece an indulgence.

Makes 32

DARK CHOCOLATE LAYER
- ☐ **410 g (13 oz) dark chocolate, broken into pieces**
- ☐ **155 g (5 oz) sweetened condensed milk**
- ☐ **30 g (1 oz) butter**
- ☐ **2 tablespoons brandy**
- ☐ **75 g (2½ oz) blanched almonds, roughly chopped and toasted**

WHITE CHOCOLATE LAYER
- ☐ **410 g (13 oz) white chocolate, broken into pieces**
- ☐ **155 g (5 oz) sweetened condensed milk**
- ☐ **30 g (1 oz) butter**
- ☐ **2 tablespoons Whisky Cream liqueur**
- ☐ **75 g (2½ oz) hazelnuts, toasted, peeled and roughly chopped**

1   To make Dark Chocolate Layer, place dark chocolate, condensed milk, butter and brandy in a saucepan and cook over a low heat, stirring constantly, until mixture is smooth and well combined. Fold in almonds and pour mixture into a 20 cm (8 in) square greased and foil-lined cake tin. Refrigerate until firm.
2   To make White Chocolate Layer, place white chocolate, condensed milk, butter and liqueur in a saucepan and cook over

a low heat, stirring constantly, until mixture is smooth and well combined. Fold in hazelnuts, cool then spread mixture over Dark Chocolate Layer. Refrigerate until firm. To serve, cut into pieces.

PASSION FRUIT PETITS FOURS

Tiny butterfly cakes flavoured with passion fruit are an impressive finish.

Makes 40
Oven temperature 180°C, 350°F, Gas 4

- ☐ 45 g (1½ oz) butter
- ☐ 1 teaspoon Grand Marnier (orange liqueur)
- ☐ 45 g (1½ oz) caster sugar
- ☐ 1 egg
- ☐ 75 g (2½ oz) self-raising flour, sifted
- ☐ 3 tablespoons passion fruit purée

TOPPING
- ☐ 125 mL (4 fl oz) doublecream, whipped
- ☐ 2 tablespoons passion fruit purée
- ☐ 2 tablespoons icing sugar, sifted

1   Place butter and Grand Marnier in a bowl and beat until creamy. Add sugar and continue beating until light and fluffy.
2   Add eggs one at a time, beating well after each addition. Fold in flour alternately with passion fruit purée.
3   Spoon mixture into petit four paper cases, placed on a baking tray. Bake for 6-8 minutes, or until cooked through and golden. Remove from oven and set

aside to cool.
4   To assemble, cut a slice from top of each cake. Halve each slice and set aside. Place cream in a piping bag fitted with a small star nozzle. Pipe top of cake with cream, position tops at an angle, back to back, in cream. Top with a little passion fruit pulp and dust lightly with icing sugar.

Left: Cheese Cigars with Coriander Pesto
Above: Chocolate Pastilles with Fruits and Nuts, Double-Indulgent Fudge, Passion Fruit Petits Fours

SURPRISE TRUFFLE BAG

A marzipan bag filled with chocolate truffles – what more spectacular way could there be to end a special dinner?

Serves 12

- ☐ **cocoa, sifted**
- ☐ **375 g (1¼ lb) marzipan**
- ☐ **1 egg white, lightly beaten**
- ☐ **2 m (2¼ yds) thin ribbon**

RICH COCONUT TRUFFLES
- ☐ **4 tablespoons sweetened condensed milk**
- ☐ **75 g (2½ oz) desiccated coconut**
- ☐ **1 tablespoon coconut liqueur**
- ☐ **200 g (6½ oz) dark chocolate, melted**

BRANDY TRUFFLES
- ☐ **200 g (6½ oz) milk chocolate, roughly chopped**
- ☐ **2 tablespoons double cream**
- ☐ **22 g (¾ oz) unsalted butter**
- ☐ **1 tablespoon brandy**
- ☐ **cocoa, sifted**

WHITE PRALINE TRUFFLES
- ☐ **200 g (6½ oz) white chocolate, roughly chopped**
- ☐ **2 tablespoons double cream**
- ☐ **22 g (¾ oz) unsalted butter**
- ☐ **90 g (3 oz) sugar**
- ☐ **3 tablespoons water**
- ☐ **30 g (1 oz) almonds**
- ☐ **icing sugar, sifted**

1 To make Rich Coconut Truffles, combine condensed milk, coconut and coconut liqueur in a bowl and mix to combine. Refrigerate until firm. Roll spoonfuls of mixture into small balls and dip in melted chocolate mixture to coat. Place on a foil-lined tray and set aside until chocolate is firm.

2 To make Brandy Truffles, place milk chocolate, cream and butter in bowl over a saucepan of simmering water, stirring, until chocolate melts and mixture is well combined. Stir in brandy. Refrigerate until firm. Roll spoonfuls of mixture into small balls and roll in cocoa. Refrigerate until required.

3 To make White Praline Truffles, place white chocolate, cream and butter in a bowl over a saucepan of simmering water, stirring, until chocolate melts and mixture is well combined. Place sugar and water in a saucepan and cook over a medium heat,

stirring constantly until sugar dissolves. Bring to the boil and continue to cook, without stirring, until golden brown. Place almonds on a greased baking tray and pour syrup over. Set aside to cool. Place praline in a food processor and process until finely chopped, but not powdered. Fold through chocolate mixture. Refrigerate until firm. Roll spoonfuls into small balls and roll in icing sugar. Refrigerate until required.

4 To make marzipan bag, dust work surface with cocoa and knead marzipan with a little egg white until it is smooth and pliable and an even chocolate colour.

5 Roll out marzipan as thinly as possible on a cocoa-dusted surface to form a large round. Place truffles in a pile in centre of marzipan and gently bring up sides of marzipan to form a neat bag. Pinch edges of crimp. Tie with a ribbon.

Dust work surface with sifted cocoa and knead marzipan with a little egg white until smooth, and an even chocolate colour.

Roll out marzipan on a cocoa-dusted surface to form a large round.

Pile truffles in centre of marzipan and gently lift sides to form a bag.

FIERY FINISHES

Flambé food is a dramatic and magnificent touch to any meal. But remember that special care is required – both in the kitchen and at the table. The flame under the pan should not be too high and you should use only a small quantity of alcohol at a time.

FLAMBE OF EXOTIC FRUITS

Use a variety of luscious fresh fruits to create an irresistible finale to your meal!

Choose from any of the following fruits:
- [ ] **pineapple and melon wedges**
- [ ] **kiwi fruit, peeled and cut into long quarters**
- [ ] **bananas, peeled and cut into 4-6 pieces**
- [ ] **apricots, stoned and cut into quarters**
- [ ] **mandarin and orange segments**
- [ ] **seedless grapes**
- [ ] **whole strawberries**
- [ ] **small bowl of alcohol of your choice, such as rum, brandy, Grand Marnier, Kirsch, Curacao or Cointreau**
- [ ] **bowl of brown sugar**
- [ ] **bowls of whipped cream**

Arrange fruit on a large platter. Each person secures a piece of fruit on a fork and dips the fruit into alcohol, then sugar and holds it over a fondue flame. When fruit caramelises, dip into cream and eat at once.

Alternative Method

1 Sprinkle fruit with sugar and dot with butter. Place fruit in a heavy-based frying pan and cook quickly until sugar melts and sauce bubbles.

2 Warm alcohol in a small saucepan, ignite and pour over fruit, shaking pan gently. Serve at once with whipped cream.

Flambe of Exotic Fruits

FLAMBE MANGOES OVER VANILLA ICE CREAM

The special combination of sweet juicy mangoes, sugar and Kirsch make up this light summery dessert. Makes your own ice cream, or buy one of the speciality brands now available, to complete this delicious dessert.

Serves 4

- ☐ **vanilla ice cream**
- ☐ **4 tablespoons caster sugar**
- ☐ **2 tablespoons Kirsch (cherry brandy)**
- ☐ **2 large ripe mangoes, stoned, peeled and sliced**

1   Spoon 4 large scoops of vanilla ice cream into four individual heatproof glass dishes. Keep frozen.

2   Place a large, heavy-based frying pan over a medium heat for 2 minutes. Add sugar and melt without stirring until it begins to caramelise. Stir until sugar is evenly caramelised.

3   Add Kirsch and ignite immediately.

Quickly stir in mangoes and cook until flames die and mangoes are heated through.

4   Spoon hot mangoes and juices over ice cream. Serve immediately.

FLAMED KIDNEYS WITH RED WINE

Serve this robust dish with hot, buttery noodles and a green salad.

Serves 4

- ☐ **750 g (1¹/₂ lb) lambs kidneys, trimmed and halved**
- ☐ **2 tablespoons seasoned flour**
- ☐ **125 g (4 oz) butter**
- ☐ **250 g (8 oz) button mushrooms, halved**
- ☐ **1 teaspoon lemon juice**
- ☐ **2 tablespoons brandy**
- ☐ **freshly ground black pepper**
- ☐ **125 mL (4 fl oz) red wine**
- ☐ **1 tablespoon finely chopped fresh parsley**

1   Place kidneys in lightly salted water and set aside to soak for 10 minutes. Drain, pat dry and chop coarsely. Toss kidneys in seasoned flour to coat.

2   Melt 75 g (2¹/₂ oz) butter in a frying pan and cook kidneys for 3 minutes over a medium-high heat, stirring with a wooden spoon. Remove kidneys using a slotted spoon, and set aside.

3   Add remaining butter to frying pan and cook mushrooms, stirring, for 4 minutes. Add lemon juice and cook until mushrooms give up most of their juices.

4   Return kidneys and any juices to pan, toss to combine, then remove from heat. Add brandy and ignite immediately. When flames die, return pan to heat and add wine. Turn heat to medium-low and cook until kidneys are tender but still pink. Season to taste with black pepper. Sprinkle with parsley and serve immediately.

COGNAC LOBSTERS WITH BASIL BUTTER

Sizzling lobster flambéd with cognac then topped with a fresh herb butter makes for a wonderfully easy and very indulgent meal.

Serves 4

- ☐ **875 g (1¾ lb) uncooked lobsters, halved and cleaned**
- ☐ **2 tablespoons lemon juice**
- ☐ **2 tablespoons olive oil**
- ☐ **freshly ground black pepper**

BASIL BUTTER

- ☐ **125 g (4 oz) butter, cubed**
- ☐ **2 tablespoons finely chopped fresh basil leaves**
- ☐ **2 teaspoons finely chopped fresh parsley**
- ☐ **freshly ground black pepper**
- ☐ **3 tablespoons cognac**

1   To make Basil Butter, beat butter until smooth. Stir in basil and parsley and season to taste with black pepper. Shape butter into a roll and wrap in greaseproof paper and refrigerate until required.

2   Sprinkle lobsters with lemon juice and brush flesh with oil. Cook under a hot grill or on a barbecue, shell side first, for 5 minutes. Turn over and cook for 5-10 minutes, or until flesh is just cooked. Brush with extra oil, if necessary, during cooking.

3   Remove lobsters from heat. Remove flesh from tails in one piece and cut into pieces. Pile back into shells and set aside to keep warm. Warm cognac, hold a lighted match over it and as soon as it ignites spoon over lobster.

4   Slice butter into four and place one slice on each lobster half. Serve immediately.

FLAMBE TIPS

❧ Alcohol must be warmed to flame effectively, however, if overheated the alcohol will evaporate before it flames.

❧ The flaming alcohol will help burn away excessive fats, dissolve the crust at the bottom of the pan and form a glaze that can become the basis of a sauce.

❧ A sprinkling of a little sugar over the food just before flaming will produce a longer lasting flame.

❧ Gently shaking the pan when the flame has been ignited will distribute both flame and alcohol, and therefore the flavour, over the food.

Left: Flambé Mangoes over Vanilla Ice Cream
Below: Flamed Kidneys with Red Wine, Cognac Lobsters with Basil Butter

PAMPERED PANTRY

Balsamic Vinegar

Balsamic vinegar is produced from the not yet fully fermented new red wine of the season. It is aged in wooden barrels to give it a distinctive almost sweet flavour and it is especially suitable for making a vinaigrette. Like any good quality vinegar, it should be transparent, not 'cloudy'. Because of its sweet flavour, balsamic vinegar is also used to dress fresh fruits and berries. In Italy well-matured balsamic vinegar is sometimes drunk as an after-dinner liqueur.

Sun-dried Tomatoes

Usually bottled, and packed in olive oil, these richly flavoured tomatoes will enhance almost any dish that requires the use of fresh tomatoes – salads, casseroles and pizza toppings. Sun-dried tomatoes once opened are best stored in the refrigerator. They are also available dried in packets from good health food stores or delicatessens.

Couverture

This refers to the chocolate coating or covering that is used for confectionery, cakes and biscuits. It is made from chocolate that has a high proportion of cocoa butter – the higher the content of cocoa butter, the richer and creamier the chocolate. Couverture can be used to cover a special gâteau and for making homemade chocolates and confectionery. As it does not require tempering it is easier to use than ordinary chocolate. Couverture is available from specialty food stores.

Oils

Studies have shown the link between heart disease and the consumption of large amounts of solid animal fats. In the interest of healthier living, the use of oils for cooking and food preparation has recently been promoted. There are many types of oils – derived from seeds, fruits and nuts. Each has its own distinctive flavour, so experiment to find those that you like best.

Sesame seed oil has a light, distinctive flavour especially suitable for Eastern dishes.

Olive oil is available in three grades: Extra Virgin, Virgin and Pure. The colour ranges from thick and green, to pale and yellow. Olive oil can be used for general cooking and is popular in salad dressings.

Nut oils such as walnut, hazelnut and almond are more expensive but their flavour is superb, and when used as the base of a vinaigrette for salad the flavour is marvellous.

Olives

Traditionally grown in the Mediterranean region, olives are now grown successfully in other parts of the world. Olives are either green (unripened) or black (ripened). Green olives are preserved in a soda solution and then pickled in brine. Black olives are preserved in brine or olive oil. Olives can be stuffed – most commonly with red pimentos. They are an excellent addition to salads, casseroles, hors d'oeuvres and antipasto platters. Store olives away from direct heat and light and serve at room temperature for the best flavour. After opening, store in the refrigerator.

Wild Rice

This dark brown to black grain with a nutty flavour is the seed from a type of grass that grows in swamp areas of the United States and Canada. The habitat in which it grows is isolated making harvesting difficult – which is reflected in its high price. Wild rice can be mixed with white and brown rice, making an eye-catching salad or tasty accompaniment.

Dried Mushrooms

These can be used in a similar way as fresh mushrooms, however, they require a little more preparation and cooking. Unlike the fresh variety that will keep for only a few days, dried mushrooms keep for months. When reconstituted, approximately 30 g (1 oz) will provide the equivalent of 250 g (8 oz) fresh mushrooms. Dried mushrooms require 15-30 minutes soaking in water before use.

There are many varieties available and they can be used as a vegetable in stir-fries, as an ingredient in a meat or poultry stuffing, or in soups.

Coconut Milk

Coconut milk and coconut cream are used in the preparation of curries, satay sauces, authentic Thai, Indian and Asian dishes. You might also like to try them instead of cow's milk when baking coconut biscuits. Once opened, canned coconut milk and coconut cream will keep in the refrigerator for only a day or two.

Coconut milk and coconut cream are interchangeable and it is easy to make your own. To make coconut milk, place 500 g (1 lb) of desiccated coconut in a bowl and add 750 mL (1¼ pt) of boiling water. Leave to stand for 30 minutes then strain, squeezing the coconut to extract as much liquid as possible. This will give a thick coconut milk or cream. The coconut can be used again to make a weaker coconut milk.

Liqueurs

The addition of a liqueur to sauces, marinades and desserts will make them just that bit more delicious. Brandy liqueurs, Grand Marnier, Cointreau, Calvados, and Amaretto all give delicious flavours. The miniature bottles now readily available in most off licences will mean that an extensive array can be amassed for a reasonable price.

USEFUL INFORMATION

In this book, ingredients such as fish and meat are given in grams so you know how much to buy. A small inexpensive set of kitchen scales is always handy and very easy to use. Other ingredients in our recipes are given in tablespoons and cups, so you will need a nest of measuring cups (1 cup, 1/2 cup, 1/3 cup and 1/4 cup), a set of measuring spoons (1 tablespoon, 1 teaspoon, 1/2 teaspoon and 1/4 teaspoon) and a transparent graduated measuring jug (1 litre or 250 mL) for measuring liquids. Cup and spoon measures are level.

OVEN TEMPERATURES

°C	°F	Gas Mark
120	250	1/2
140	275	1
150	300	2
160	325	3
180	350	4
190	375	5
200	400	6
220	425	7
240	475	8
250	500	9

QUICK CONVERTER

Metric	Imperial
5 mm	1/4 in
1 cm	1/2 in
2 cm	3/4 in
2.5 cm	1 in
5 cm	2 in
10 cm	4 in
15 cm	6 in
20 cm	8 in
23 cm	9 in
25 cm	10 in
30 cm	12 in

MEASURING DRY INGREDIENTS

Metric	Imperial
15 g	1/2 oz
30 g	1 oz
60 g	2 oz
90 g	3 oz
125 g	4 oz
155 g	5 oz
185 g	6 oz
220 g	7 oz
250 g	8 oz
280 g	9 oz
315 g	10 oz
375 g	12 oz
410 g	13 oz
440 g	14 oz
470 g	15 oz
500 g	16 oz (1 lb)
750 g	1 lb 8 oz
1 kg	2 lb
1.5 kg	3 lb

MEASURING LIQUIDS

Metric	Imperial	Cup
30 mL	1 fl oz	
60 mL	2 fl oz	1/4 cup
90 mL	3 fl oz	
125 mL	4 fl oz	1/2 cup
155 mL	5 fl oz	
170 mL	5 1/2 fl oz	2/3 cup
185 mL	6 fl oz	
220 mL	7 fl oz	
250 mL	8 fl oz	1 cup
500 mL	16 fl oz	2 cups
600 mL	20 fl oz (1 pt)	
750 mL	1 1/4 pt	
1 litre	1 3/4 pt	4 cups
1.2 litres	2 pt	

METRIC CUPS & SPOONS

Metric	Cups	Imperial
60 mL	1/4 cup	2 fl oz
80 mL	1/3 cup	2 1/2 fl oz
125 mL	1/2 cup	4 fl oz
250 mL	1 cup	8 fl oz
	Spoons	
1.25 mL	1/4 teaspoon	
2.5 mL	1/2 teaspoon	
5 mL	1 teaspoon	
20 mL	1 tablespoon	

INDEX

ACKNOWLEDGEMENTS
The publishers wish to thank the following Admiral
Appliances; Black & Decker (Australasia) Pty Ltd;
Blanco Appliances; Knebel Kitchens; Leigh Mardon
Pty Ltd; Master Foods of Australia; Meadow Lea
Foods; Namco Cookware; Ricegrowers' Co-op Mills
Ltd; Sunbeam Corporation Ltd; Tycraft Pty Ltd
distributors of Braun, Australia; White Wings Foods for
their assistance during recipe testing.

Penny Cook for her assistance during recipe testing.

COVER
Ashley Mackevicius (photography), Wendy Berecry
(Styling). Plates and cup from Royal Doulton.